Fodor's 92 Disney World & the Orlando Area

Fodor's Travel Publications, Inc.
New York and London

ISBN 0-679-02035-7

Chapter 2 © 1968, 1985 by Richard Schickel

Fodor's Disney World & the Orlando Area

Editor: Caroline V. Haberfeld
Editorial Contributors: Mike Etzkin, Amanda B. Jacobs
Art Director: Fabrizio La Rocca
Cartographer: David Lindroth
Illustrator: Karl Tanner
Cover Photograph: Jeff Foott/Bruce Colemann

Design: Vignelli Associates

Special Sales

Fodor's Travel Publications are available at special discounts for bulk purchases (100 copies or more) for sales promotions or premiums. Special editions, including personalized covers, excerpts of existing guides, and corporate imprints, can be created in large quantities for special needs. For more information write to Special Marketing, Fodor's Travel Publications, 201 E. 50th Street, New York, NY 10022; or call 800/800–3246. Inquiries from the United Kingdom should be sent to Fodor's Travel Publications, 20 Vauxhall Bridge Rd., London SW1V 2SA.

MANUFACTURED IN THE UNITED STATES OF AMERICA
10 9 8 7 6 5 4 3 2 1

Contents

Foreword

While every care has been taken to ensure the accuracy of the information in this guide, the passage of time will always bring change, and consequently the publisher cannot accept responsibility for errors that may occur.

All prices and opening times quoted here are based on information available to us at press time. Hours and admission fees may change, however, and the prudent traveler will avoid inconvenience by calling ahead.

Fodor's wants to hear about your travel experiences, both pleasant and unpleasant. When a hotel or restaurant fails to live up to its billing, let us know and we will investigate the complaint and revise our entries where the facts warrant it.

Send your letters to the editors of Fodor's Travel Publications, 201 E. 50th Street, New York, NY 10022.

Highlights'92 and Fodor's Choice

Highlights '92

Pardon the pixie dust, but Disney World and the Orlando area are flying high in an era of expansion.

If you haven't been to Orlando in a couple of years, and you are flying in, the first change you will notice will be at Orlando International Airport. It has added a third terminal, a third runway, two six-story parking garages, and an expanded international arrivals concourse. A fourth runway is on the drawing boards to help accommodate the 21 million travelers who use the airport each year.

The Disney decade began with expansion at Disney-MGM Studios Theme Park, which will more than double the size of the 110-acre park. New shows have already been added and the **Muppet Studios** should be open beginning this year. Two restaurants and a 3-D movie are also planned. Next on the Disney drawing board is a Muppets movie ride, a nighttime show, *Noah's Ark*, being developed by *Phantom of the Opera* creator Andrew Lloyd Webber. It will be presented on the waterway connecting Epcot Center and Disney-MGM. In the mid-1990s, **Sunset Boulevard** is scheduled to be completed, including Dick Tracy's Crime Stoppers, a ride in which visitors will be able to shoot Tommy guns during a high-speed chase; Mickey's Movieland, a replica of Walt Disney's original studios; a Toontown Trolley, another one of those popular flight-simulator rides, this one through the world of Roger Rabbit.

In Epcot Center, work is scheduled to begin this year on **Journeys in Space,** a space exploration pavillion in the Future World portion of the park. Other Disney decade enhancements won't come on line until the mid-1990s, but look for a new 3-D musical movie by *Star Wars* creator George Lucas, followed by two new pavillions in World Showcase: Switzerland, with a Matterhorn Mountain thrill ride, and the U.S.S.R.

The most notable change in the Magic Kingdom this year will be its new 360° Circlevision show on the cultures of Western civilization. Next year should see **Splash Mountain,** a replica of the popular water ride in Disneyland that features a five-story plunge. In all, seven major attractions will be added to the Magic Kingdom before 2000. Two of the new attractions will be an outerspace musical revue and Alien Encounter, in which a space visitor will terrorize the audience. The Magic Kingdom has already added a live stage show in Tomorrowland Theater, a new character show in Mickey's Starland, and a musical salute to favorite Disney films.

Universal Studios Florida proved a big hit despite technical difficulties with many of its major rides in the opening year.

Back to the Future, a new ride using flight simulators, a large screen, and special effects, should be ready for visitors by the end of 1991, and Jaws, one of the original rides that never worked properly, should be back to scare you in '92.

Around the entrance to Universal Studios Florida, some old favorites are going through a face-lift. Among them is Twin Towers Hotel, now completely outlined in neon. The 760-room hotel completed its $29 million renovation to its convention center, refurbished its guest rooms, added a new executive business center, concierge floors, a restaurant, a deli, a lounge, and a pool bar. Delta Orlando Resort, formerly the Delta Court of Flags, went through a $6 million upgrade, including the remodeling of all 800 rooms. Mystery Fun House completed a $200,000 project that spruced up the attraction and added a walk-through adventure with earthquake sensations.

Sea World introduced two new shows: "10,000 BC," with a sea lion and otter; and "Shamu: New Visions," with its star killer whale and underwater cameras. Shortly after Anheuser-Busch purchased Sea World two years ago, it made plans for a working brewery and tour by 1992.

Among the **dinner theaters** that come and go in Orlando, For Liberty Wild West Dinner Show & Trading Post recently went through a $25 million expansion, adding a wax museum and shops. The year before, Medieval Times expanded by adding Raimonburg, a village featuring demonstrations by artisans.

Visitors will shortly be able to see a dramatic **Astronauts Memorial** at Kennedy Space Center's Spaceport USA. The memorial will honor American astronauts who lost their lives in the line of duty. A 42-foot polished granite monument will have a rotating space mirror that projects the astronauts' names into the sky.

There is good news for visitors who want to stay on Disney property without paying the high prices. Prompted by the success of Disney's moderately priced Caribbean Beach Resort, WDW immediately went to work on its Mississippi River hotels. **Port Orleans Resort,** designed to capture the flavor of New Orleans's French Quarter, should be open by 1992 and will offer 1,008 rooms. It will have two major dining areas; the French Market, with a variety of vendors serving up everything from pralines to shrimp gumbo; and a shaded courtyard café serving Southern-style French cuisine. A winding river road and a waterway will connect Port Orleans to Dixie Landings Resort, which is scheduled to be completed this year. Dixie Landings will provide 2,048 moderately priced rooms in two settings—four three-story, plantation-style mansions in one village, and two-story bayou dwellings in another. The plantation houses will be surrounded by formal gardens, and the weathered-wood, tin-roofed bayou buildings will be in a swamplike setting. Dining options at Dixie Landing will include the Plantation Marketplace, which will be family dining down by the old mill stream in an open courtyard, and Bayou Bill's Cafe, featuring catfish, corn fritters, and other Cajun treats. The two resorts, located between Epcot Center and the Disney Village marketplace on the Lake Buena Vista golf course, will share seven swimming pools, a children's play area, arcades, and retail shops. The hotels will be linked by waterway to the Disney Village Marketplace and Pleasure Island and by bus to Disney-MGM, Epcot Center, Magic Kingdom, Typhoon Lagoon, and Pleasure Island.

At the other end of the scale, the Mediterranean Resort, 1,000 luxury rooms on the Seven Seas Lagoon near the Magic Kingdom, is scheduled for completion at the end of this year.

Other hotel projects on the books: by the mid-'90s, Wilderness Lodge (700 rooms) and Buffalo Junction (600 rooms) both near Fort Wilderness Campground; by the late '90s, Disney Kingdom Suites (200 rooms) near the Magic Kingdom; Disney Boardwalk Resort (530 luxury suites) on the Boardwalk with the Epcot Center hotels; and two Hollywood-style hotels with 1,000 rooms each, including Hollywood Horror Hotel, with its "tower of terror" and other haunted rooms to tour. The Orlando area last year boasted the highest number of hotel rooms (more than 76,000) in the country. By the year 2000, WDW alone will be offering 21,000 rooms. What is even more extraordinary is that those hotel rooms averaged 80% occupancy.

Thunder and Lightning will be coming Orlando's way in 1992. The Orlando Thunder team is a member of the new World League of American Football, which plays a spring–summer schedule. The Thunder will play home games at the 70,000-seat Citrus Bowl. The National Hockey League awarded Tampa an expansion team, The Lightning, to begin play in 1992. They are expected to play their first season at the 15,000-seat Orlando Arena, while Tampa's new ice house is being built.

Besides Thunder and Lightning, there will be more than the usual slammin' and jammin' at the O-rena, home of the National Basketball Association's Orlando Magic. Orlando will play host February 7–9 to the NGA All-Star weekend festivities.

Fodor's Choice

No two people will agree on what makes a perfect vacation, but it's fun and helpful to know what others think. We hope you'll have a chance to experience some of Fodor's Choices yourself while visiting Disney World and the Orlando Area. For detailed information about each entry, refer to the appropriate chapters in this guidebook.

Lodging

Hilton at Walt Disney World Village
(Expensive–Very Expensive)

Chalet Suzanne *(Moderate–Expensive)*

Park Plaza Hotel *(Moderate–Expensive)*

Ramada Resort Maingate East at the Parkway *(Moderate)*

Casa Rosa Inn *(Inexpensive)*

Dining

Chalet Suzanne *(Expensive)*

Dux *(Expensive)*

Chatham's Place *(Moderate–Expensive)*

Jordan's Grove *(Moderate–Expensive)*

Spinnaker's *(Moderate–Expensive)*

Le Coq au Vin *(Moderate)*

Sweet Basil *(Moderate)*

Rolandos *(Inexpensive)*

Walt Disney World Attractions

Jungle Cruise (Magic Kingdom)

The Main Street Electrical Parade (Magic Kingdom)

Pirates of the Caribbean (Magic Kingdom)

Space Mountain (Magic Kingdom)

Body Wars (Future World, Epcot)

Spaceship Earth (Future World, Epcot)

IllumiNations (World Showcase, Epcot)

Norway's Maelstrom (World Showcase, Epcot)

Wonders of China (World Showcase, Epcot)

Epic Stunt Spectacular (Disney-MGM)

The Great Movie Ride (Disney-MGM)

Star Tours (Disney-MGM)

Attractions Outside Walt Disney World

Sharks! (Sea World)

Der Stuka water slide (Wet 'n Wild)

Spaceport USA

United States Astronaut Hall of Fame

Shuttle launches

Off the Beaten Track

Charles Hosmer Morse Museum of American Art

Bok Tower Gardens

Nightlife

Church Street Station

J.J. Whispers

Shopping

Belz Factory Outlet

Bountiful Harvest (China Pavilion, Epcot)

Mickey's Character Shop (WDW Shopping Village)

Park Avenue

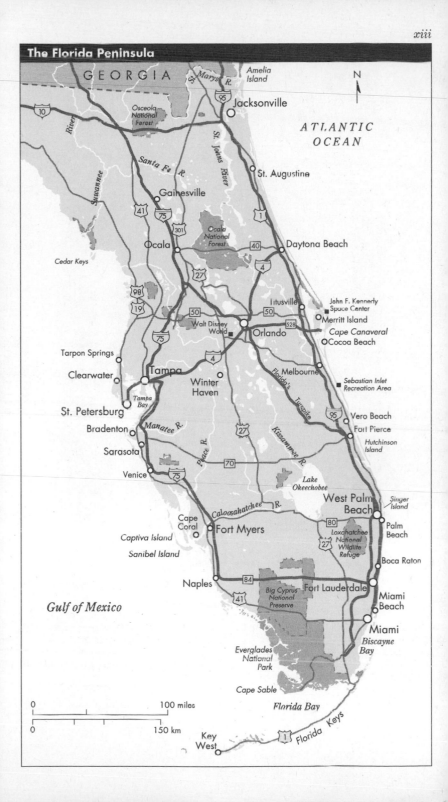

The Florida Peninsula

GEORGIA

Amelia Island

Jacksonville

ATLANTIC OCEAN

Osceola National Forest

St. Augustine

Gainesville

Ocala

Ocala National Forest

Daytona Beach

Cedar Keys

Titusville

John F. Kennedy Space Center

Merritt Island

Cape Canaveral

Cocoa Beach

Walt Disney World

Orlando

Tarpon Springs

Clearwater

Tampa

Winter Haven

Melbourne

Sebastian Inlet Recreation Area

St. Petersburg

Tampa Bay

Bradenton

Manatee R.

Vero Beach

Fort Pierce

Hutchinson Island

Sarasota

Venice

Lake Okeechobee

West Palm Beach

Singer Island

Cape Coral

Fort Myers

Caloosahatchee R.

Loxahatchee National Wildlife Refuge

Palm Beach

Captiva Island

Sanibel Island

Boca Raton

Naples

Big Cypress National Preserve

Fort Lauderdale

Miami Beach

Gulf of Mexico

Miami

Biscayne Bay

Everglades National Park

Cape Sable

Florida Bay

0   100 miles

0   150 km

Key West

Florida Keys

St. Marys R.

Santa Fe R.

St. Johns River

River

Suwannee

Florida's Turnpike

Kissimmee R.

Peace R.

N

World Time Zones

Numbers below vertical bands relate each zone to Greenwich Mean Time (0 hrs.).
Local times frequently differ from these general indications,
as indicated by light-face numbers on map.

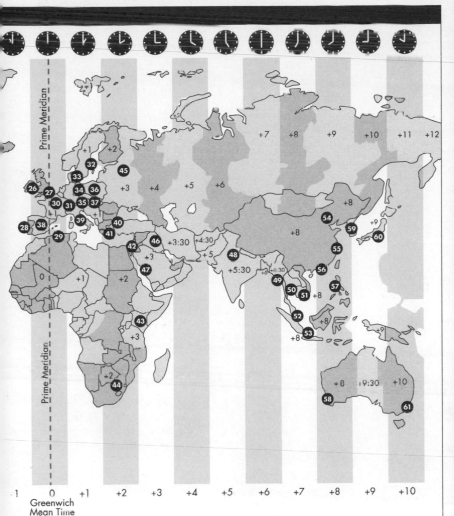

Introduction

by Karen Cure

Ms. Cure, whose favorite ride is the Haunted Mansion, writes extensively on Walt Disney World.

Millions of visitors, even those who place Pirates of the Caribbean and Space Mountain among the wonders of the world, right up there with the Eiffel Tower and the Pyramids, can't accurately define Walt Disney World.

The sheer size of the property—27,400 acres near Kissimmee, Florida—suggests that WDW is more than a single theme park, a Disneyland clone, with a fabulous castle in the center and the most dazzling rides on earth. The 27,400 acres translate to 43 square miles—twice the size of Manhattan or Bermuda, 60 times larger than Monaco, and just a shade smaller than Nantucket or Liechtenstein. If you were to drive at 60 miles per hour from one side of the property to the other, it would take close to three-quarters of an hour. On a tract that size, 98 acres is a mere speck, yet that is the size of the Magic Kingdom. When most people imagine Walt Disney World, they think only of those 98 acres, but in actuality there is much, much more. Some 2,500 acres of the 27,400 are occupied by hotels and villa complexes, each with its own theme and each equipped with recreational facilities like swimming pools and golf courses. All of these are part of Walt Disney World. Epcot Center, a little over twice the size of the Magic Kingdom, is the second major theme park. Devoted to exploring the world as it is today and may be in the future, it, too, is within the boundaries of Walt Disney World. In 1989, the Disney-MGM Studios, devoted to the doings of the film business, opened nearby, along with a new villa complex. And all of that is inside Walt Disney World.

In addition, there are thousands of acres of undeveloped property—grassy plains and pine forests patrolled by deer, and swamps patched by thickets of palmettos and fluttering with white ibis—even now, almost 20 years after opening day. When you take a Walt Disney World exit off I-4 or U.S. 192 and begin traveling across empty land devoid of billboards or any other promotional materials, you're in Walt Disney World, even though there's not a Cinderella Castle in sight. It's a very, very big place.

To understand how this all came to be, it helps to go back to the beginnings of the Disney theme park organization in Anaheim, California, at Disneyland.

When it opened in 1956, amusement parks were widely considered dinosaurs of their species, a vanishing breed, cultural anachronisms. The 17th- and 18th-century European pleasure gardens where families strolled tree-lined paths between flower beds, marveled at balloon ascensions and trapeze acts, and enjoyed musical presentations—

places like England's Vauxhall Gardens and Vienna's 2,000-acre Prater, with its Ferris wheel, Russian mountains, fun houses—had given way to parks full of thrill rides. After World War II, these were abandoned by the family trade and taken over by hoodlums, staffed by sinister carnival types, and maintained poorly. What Walt Disney saw when he tried to take his daughters there were overflowing trash bins, trampled gardens, peeling paint.

While munching popcorn on a bench in one of them one day, he got the idea to build a "magical little park" for families. He persuaded his brother Roy, financial manager of his studio operation, to let him use $10,000, then borrowed on his life insurance to buy up the surrounding orange groves, and gathered a staff of "imagineers" to design the park. His colleagues and friends made gloomy predictions about what they thought of as "Walt's screwy ideas." But Disneyland, publicized on the then-nascent ABC network's weekly Disneyland show, was an instant hit, and soon the orange groves on its perimeters were sprouting motels, restaurants, and other tourist facilities, and people were traveling from all over the country to experience the phenomenon. By the end of its first decade, the number of attractions had grown from 22 to 47, the investment from $17 million to $48 million.

Walt was increasingly disturbed at the commercialization on the park's perimeter. "Believe me," he said, "if I ever build another Disneyland, I would make sure I could control the class and the theme of the enterprises around it."

At the same time, he was dreaming of a new community to show how people could live together happily in a pleasant environment.

Perhaps, he thought, a second Disneyland park would be its "weenie," the term he always used to describe something that attracted and held the interest of his visitors, the designer's answer to the carnie barker. The City of Tomorrow would be all around it. And that was how Walt Disney World developed.

As early as 1958 Walt was evaluating possible sites, and in 1959 he settled on Florida—inland Florida, away from hurricanes, salt spray, and the frivolities of the beach—and began the lengthy process of acquiring the land. The Magic Kingdom as he envisioned it, the weenie, more or less replicated the California property, with a few minor differences. As for the surrounding land, it preoccupied Disney, who called it EPCOT, an Experimental Prototype Community of Tomorrow.

In the City of Tomorrow that Disney was planning, there would be no slums, no landowning (only rentals at modest rates), no retirees (only working people). It would build upon new ideas and new technologies, and it would always be introducing, testing, and demonstrating new systems and new materials. It would be "a showcase . . . of the ingenuity and imagination of American free enterprise," and it would never be completed.

Disney himself sketched out sites of hotels, lakes, campgrounds, and entrances for visitors and service vehicles in this EPCOT, this City of Tomorrow. But in 1966, a week after plans for the "new Disneyland" were publicly announced on the Disneyland television show, he died.

His brother and partner of forty years, Roy O. Disney, carried on without him, and when the new Disney creation opened five years later he named it *Walt* Disney World in acknowledgment of the man who gave it life; among those who know the place well, the name has stuck and is never shortened to the popular "Disney World." Roy died a year later, and the company remained under the leadership of longtime Disney executives—most recently Ron Miller, the husband of Walt's daughter Diane—until 1984, when former Paramount president Michael Eisner took the helm after nine months of well-publicized takeover attempts and concomitant intramural turmoil. But as Disney himself decreed, WDW has never been completed; as one new confection is welcoming its first guests, another is beginning construction and still others are under study.

Many observers say that Epcot Center, the Disney project that opened in 1982, is merely an overblown commercial enterprise, a travesty of Walt's original vision of his EPCOT. This critique misses the point. Disney's plans to develop a ski slope on prime southern California forestland foundered on environmentalists' protests just before Epcot Center got underway, so Epcot's genesis may have had as much to do with Walt's dream as it did with a corporate cash surplus—nobody ever accused the Disney organization of being impervious to financial realities. Nonetheless, Epcot Center did turn out as the "showcase of technology" that Walt envisioned: Technology is the subject of many of the exhibits, particularly in Future World, and, more to the point, Epcot Center is state-of-the-art to its core, from the ticket-taking system to the complex computerized irrigation system, as is Walt Disney World in its entirety.

More than 15 years later, Walt Disney World still incorporates many facets of its founder's vision of a state-of-the-art settlement, an experimental prototype community of tomorrow. Though it still has no permanent residents, it does have an enormous transient population and a year-round staff numbering 20,000—more in peak periods. As a result, the Disney organization faces many of the same responsibilities that challenge the ingenuity of business and society in the outside world. And the company's distinctive responses to those challenges have earned it a reputation as an innovator.

The transportation system that serves the 43-square-mile property—buses, boats, monorail trains—manages to be decidedly pleasant as it moves millions around the property in comfort with astonishing speed. The monorail is the largest commercial transport of its kind in the world, and has moved 750 million visitors in Walt Disney World since it opened in 1971. Still, the cars look as new as the day they were built.

Utilities and other service facilities are below ground in "utilidors" so that excavations like those that pothole streets in New York and other cities are unnecessary.

Trash and waste disposal is high art, as might be expected on a property spawned by the fastidious Walt Disney (who, in Disneyland, personally patrolled the grounds in search of the single burned-out light bulb or the rare overflowing trash bin). Today at Walt Disney World, cast members from the maintenance department, in costumes appropriate to the area of WDW for which they are responsible, cover their assigned territory several times an hour. The whole system is engineered to make it easy for both staff and guests to dispose properly of trash. The ultimate receptacles are high-speed, high-tech pneumatic tubes that feed a central collection plant; the same system is now used on Roosevelt Island, off the eastern shore of Manhattan. As for waste, it's incinerated, filtered, and water-scrubbed to the point that only steam leaves the smokestack. Sewage is turned into potable water at a tertiary treatment plant or treated by ponds filled with water hyacinths, which remove the impurities; it's then used for irrigation.

In an age in which rising costs of liability insurance are shutting down municipal parks, a lesson can be learned from the safety consciousness of Disney's organization—averting accidents before they occur. Pressure-sensitive areas beneath or alongside ride vehicles in many attractions automatically shut down the system when a wayward guest gets out of the car (say, to retrieve a dropped camera). In Space Mountain, infrared cameras that can see in the dark are placed at strategic points above the tracks and monitored by a full crew, who stop the ride if any guest attempts something dangerous. The clean-swept streets are as much a matter of safety as of appearance. When accidents do occur, as is inevitable in the presence of millions of visitors a year, cast members offer a soft shoulder and then call on supervisors and security hosts, who get the facts from witnesses and the injured and write everything down. As a result, Disney hardly ever loses a personal injury case.

In employee and customer relations, the Walt Disney Company is also a leader, and was cited as such by Thomas J. Peters and Robert H. Waterman, Jr., in the best-selling *In Search of Excellence: Lessons from America's Best-Run Companies*. The Disney canon pronounces each employee a "cast member," part of the "show"; the pervasive attitude is that happy employees help make happy visitors and that bit parts are as important as starring roles. The day-long Traditions I course, part of a multiday program for new cast members, teaches about the company's history and goals and demonstrates with tours of the property how all the divisions function together to create the big show that is Walt Disney World. The organization lets cast members feel they matter in tangible ways as well. In addition to health insurance, the company pays for job-related educational programs in which cast members want to enroll and sponsors still others for college credit, organizes car pools for cast members who want them, sponsors two on-the-property child care facilities that keep the same long and unusual hours that employees themselves often do, and owns and maintains a pretty lake with beach and picnic and play areas for cast members and their families. On the job, each cast member is given the emotional support and the physical equipment he or she needs to get the job done. For instance, when the costumed characters make appearances in the park, they're accompanied by walkie-talkie-wielding colleagues in business attire—protection against the occasional over-eager guest. Finally, so that management never loses track of the challenges faced by the cast members "on-stage," executives do annual "cross-utilization" stints loading rides, parking cars, serving food, and otherwise experiencing the frontline jobs. According to Peters and Waterman, such corporate emphasis on the importance of the customer and the concomitant view of the rank and file as a prime source of corporate quality and productivity are the hallmarks of America's best-run companies.

T he Disney organization is equally adept at handling crowds without dehumanizing individuals. For example, Richard Schickel, author of *The Disney Version,* a thoughtful study of Walt's art and commerce, commends the handling of queues as "a marvel of technology applied to mass psychology . . . well worth the study of anybody faced with the problem of creating structures to serve large numbers of people comfortably but with no loss of efficient revenue production." The Magic Kingdom is one of "the most intelligently conceived pieces of architecture in America." Many queues snake through rope-and-stanchion mazes arranged so as to provide a changing view of humanity and keep guests entertained; when lines are particularly long, strolling entertainers are dispatched. In the Magic Kingdom's Big Thunder Mountain Railroad and Space Mountain, the queue is part of the show: To establish just the right mood, the line at the former snakes between reddish man-made boulders fuzzed by real desert plants, past a rushing stream, and underneath the tracks at a point at which all aboard are squealing with mixed terror and delight; inside Space Mountain, where all is dark, waiting passengers can only speculate on the cause of the screams as they watch the "shooting stars" and "meteorites" overhead and listen to the rumbling and clattering of the "rockets" on the tracks. The suspense is exquisite. Throughout WDW, footpaths are wide enough for crowds but seem intimate as well because they're seldom straight-as-an-arrow. The curves set the tone for a visit: They suggest strolling and, by design, encourage guests to slow down and smell the flowers. And when eager visitors both young and old race pell-mell to their favorite attraction after a theme park's morning opening, you can't help but think of pressured Manhattan executives racing for a rushhour subway car before the doors close; the whole scene seems curiously at odds with the environment, which is one of ease, relaxation, pleasure.

Walt Disney's City of Tomorrow, a community where people would actually live, still does not exist per se; even now it is no further than the discussion stages, and the Epcot Center that now exists is still only a *center*, a focal point. But Walt Disney World as a whole has evolved as an experimental community that is very close to Walt's dream; and the visual representations of future communities as seen in Future World's Horizons pavilion and the light-spangled model city-in-the-dark in World of Motion are less to the point than how it feels to work at Disney or to be a guest of the Disney organization in one of its theme parks or hotels.

No matter which point of view you take, the place is very grand. From the gardens full of birds and butterflies, bamboo thickets, and topiary statues, to the lakes thrumming with motorboats and the shops brimming over with treasures and trinkets that sometimes seem irresistible, every detail is as highly polished as a Disney film. In the hotels, wake-up calls come when they're supposed to, room-service breakfasts are delivered on time with no missing pieces, and at the end of a visit the bill appears under the door; if it's accurate, you don't even need to check out. The Disney experience swings between poles—the sheer fun of the Magic Kingdom or of song-and-dance shows like Fort Wilderness' Hoop-Dee-Doo-Revue to the interesting and handsomely presented displays of Epcot Center, which is informative enough not to bore but never so intellectually taxing that you forget you're on vacation. There is plenty of music everywhere, and it's nearly always tuneful. (You can just imagine Walt saying to the bandleader, as he once did in Disneyland, "I don't want to hear you playing anything that I can't walk away humming.") The stray gum wrapper on the sidewalk always comes as a surprise. You can relax, stop fighting the battles of life in the real world, and let yourself be seduced by the prettiness and pleasantness of it all.

Only after the thrill and the novelty of it all wears off do you begin to wonder, "So what? What about the crises of cities today? Can Mickey Mouse transform the slums, educate the disadvantaged, repair rifts in drug-torn families, solve the crisis in health care aggravated by AIDS?" Walt himself once declined a suggestion, by science fiction author Ray Bradbury, that he run for mayor of Los Angeles. Why should I run for mayor, Walt is reported to have said, when I'm already king?

In fact, the very desire to create a Disneyland or a Walt Disney World suggests he knew how hard it would be to control complex issues in the real world. It may be that Walt was not thinker enough to grapple with them. Or it may be that he never meant to address them at all, at least at Walt Disney World; that he intended simply to sketch a direction for the future in the broadest possible strokes and to structure a situation in which certain new technologies could have their day in the sun.

Certainly, on those terms, Walt Disney World is a great success. Visiting any portion of Walt Disney World, you can't help but wish that more airlines, government agencies, and other organizations that serve the public did the job as well as WDW, that more of them equated public safety and cleanliness with profits, that more employers would even give lip service to making their employees feel appreciated, or, even better, that they understood that good employee relations can be good business.

In the meantime, as you take a heart-stopping swoop through the star-glittering galaxy of the Magic Kingdom's Space Mountain, or, in Epcot Center, sit under the shade of a Callary pear tree frosted with blooms, or inspect the rose gardens flourishing in the shadow of Canada, or watch the gyrations of the belly dancer's belly in the cool Moroccan courtyard, or gasp at yet another massive explosion of unbelievable pyrotechnics in the IllumiNations fireworks and laser show, the pleasure of the moment is more than enough.

1 Essential Information

Before You Go

Visitor Information

Visitors to Mickey's realm should direct all inquiries to **Walt Disney World,** Box 10040, Lake Buena Vista, FL 32830. Attention: Guest letters. Tel. 407/824–4321. Request a free copy of the *Walt Disney World Vacation Guide.* For accommodations, *see* Lodging chapter.

For information on the Greater Orlando area, contact the **Tourist Information Center,** 8445 International Dr., Orlando, FL 32819, tel. 407/363–5800. Open daily 8–8. Ask for the free *Discover Orlando* guidebook.

Visitors to the Kissimmee area on U.S. 192 can get brochures from the **Kissimmee/St. Cloud Convention and Visitors' Bureau,** 1925 E. Irlo Bronson Hwy., Kissimmee, FL 34744, tel. 407/847–5000 (Kissimmee), 407/423–6070 (Orlando); in FL, 800/432–9199, outside FL, 800/327–9159.

Tour Groups

The vast majority of Disney-bound travelers opt for independent rather than group packages. With so many rental cars and buses to and from Orlando attractions, getting around is easy enough on your own. Choosing a package will depend mostly on your pocketbook. As a general rule, the farther the hotel is from Disney's front door, the less expensive it will be. Quality ranges from roadside motels to gleaming new resort-style hotels—as usual, you get what you pay for.

When considering a tour, be sure to find out (1) exactly what expenses are included, particularly tips, taxes, sidetrips, additional meals, and entertainment; (2) ratings of all hotels on the itinerary and the facilities they offer; (3) cancellation policies for both you and for the tour operator; and (4) if you are traveling alone, what the single supplement is. Most tour operators request that bookings be made through a travel agent—there is no additional charge for doing so.

General-Interest Tours **Globus-Gateway/Cosmos** (150 S. Los Robles Ave., Suite 860, Pasadena, CA 91101, tel. 818/449–0919 or 800/556–5454) offers a comprehensive eight-day tour that includes entry to Disney World. If you live in the eastern half of the country, **Domenico Tours** (751 Broadway, Bayonne, NJ 07002, tel. 201/823–8687 or 800/554–TOUR) will take you to Orlando via tour bus or direct flight; from the West it's air only.

Cruises

Carnival Cruise Lines runs three- and four-day cruises to the Bahamas aboard *Carnivale. Tel. 800/327–9501.*

Europa Cruise Line operates 6-hour cruises into the Atlantic Ocean. The *Europa Star* has cruises on Sunday from 1 to 7 PM, Monday–Wednesday, Friday, and Saturday 10 AM–4 PM, and Thursday–Saturday 7 PM–1 AM. There is dining, dancing, live entertainment, and a casino. *Europa Cruise Line, Box 1018, Cape Canaveral, 32920, tel. 800/688–PLAY.*

The Grand Romance, a replica of an old-time sidewheeler that used to cruise the inland waterways, has either three- or four-hour cruises daily beginning at 10 AM, plus a romantic dinner-dance cruise Friday and Saturday evenings, and a RiverDaze Revue dinner and show Tuesday–Thursday. Prices range from $26.25 to $40, depending on the cruise; children 12 and under travel for half-price. Reservations are required. *433 N. Palmetto Ave., Sanford, 32771, tel. in U.S., 800/225-7999, in FL, 407/321-5091 or 800/423-7401.*

Premier Cruise Lines offer Walt Disney World packages that combine with its regular 3- or 4-night cruises to the Bahamas aboard their Star/Ships *Atlantic, Majestic,* and *Oceanic. Box 573, Cape Canaveral, 32920, tel. 407/452-2810; 800/366-1268 or 800/327-7113, in FL.*

Package Deals for Independent Travelers

American Express Vacations (Box 5014, Atlanta, GA 30302, tel. 800/637-6200 or 800/282-0800 in Ga) gives you a choice of dozens of hotels (at a wide range of prices) in its independent packages, some at Walt Disney World Vacation Resort and WDW Village, others in nearby areas. **American Fly AAway Vacations** (tel. 800/321-2121) offers some packages to Florida, including admission to Disney World, Sea World, hotel packages and car rentals. **Delta Dream Vacations,** through Certified Tours (tel. 800/872-7786 or 800/221-6666), has packages that put you in Disney-owned hotels, with a four-day pass and choice of midsize car rental or free transfers. **SuperCities** (7855 Haskell Ave., Van Nuys, CA 91406, tel. 818/988-6774 or 800/556-5660) offers accommodations and car rental or transfers, plus admission to the Magic Kingdom, EPCOT, Disney-MGM Studios Theme Park, Sea World, and evening dinner attractions. **GoGo Tours** (69 Spring St., Ramsey, NJ 07446, tel. 201/934-3500 or 800/526-5047) includes choice of hotel and discounts to Orlando attractions in its package plans. Other reliable operators include: **TWA Getaway Vacations** (tel. 800/GETAWAY), **Continental Airlines** (tel. 800/634-5555) and **United Airlines** (tel. 800/328-6877).

Tips for British Travelers

Tourist Offices Direct inquiries to **Walt Disney Co.** (20th Century House, 31–32 Soho Sq., London W1V 6AP, tel. 071/734-8111).

For travel outside Disney World, contact the **U.S. Travel and Tourism Administration** (22 Sackville St., London W1X 2EA, tel. 071/439-7433).

Passports and Visas You will need a valid, 10-year passport (cost £15) to enter the USA. You do not need a visa so long as you are visiting either on business or pleasure; are staying for less than 90 days; have a return ticket; are flying with a major airline (in effect, all airlines that fly to the USA); and a complete visa waiver form I791 (supplied either at the airport of departure or on the plane and to be handed in on arrival). Otherwise, you can obtain a visa from your travel agent or by post from the U.S. Embassy, Visa and Immigration Dept., 5 Upper Grosvenor St., London W1A 2JB, tel. 071/499-3443 recorded message or 071/499-7010. The embassy no longer accepts visa applications in person. No vaccinations are required for entry into the USA.

Customs Visitors 21 and over can take in 200 cigarettes *or* 50 cigars *or* 2 kilograms of tobacco; 1 liter of alcohol; and duty-free gifts to a value of $100. Don't try to take in meat or meat products, seeds, plants, fruits, etc. Avoid illegal drugs like the plague.

Returning to Britain you can bring home: (1) 200 cigarettes *or* 100 cigarillos *or* 50 cigars *or* 250 grams of tobacco; (2) two liters of table wine with additional allowances for (a) one liter of alcohol over 22% by volume (most spirits) or (b) two liters of alcohol under 22% by volume (fortified or sparkling wine) or (c) two more liters of table wine; (3) 60 milliliters of perfume and 250 milliliters of toilet water; and (4) other goods up to a value of £32, but no more than 50 liters of beer or 25 lighters.

Insurance We recommend that you insure yourself against sickness and motoring mishaps with **Europ Assistance,** 252 High St., Croydon, Surrey CR0 1NF, tel. 081/680–1234. It is also wise to take out insurance to cover lost luggage (though check to see whether you are already covered through your existing homeowner's policy) and trip cancellation. The **Association of British Insurers** (Aldermary House, 10–15 Queen St., London EC4N 1TT, tel. 071/248–4477) will give comprehensive advice on all aspects of vacation insurance.

Tour Operators Among the many companies offering packages to Disney World and the Orlando area are:

American Airplan (Airplan House, Churchfield Rd., Walton-on-Thames, Surrey KT12 2TZ, tel. 0932/231322) offers a wide range of options, such as car rental, inclusive Freestyle holidays, self-catering apartments and two-center packages.

Cosmosair (Ground Floor, Dale House, Tiviot Dale, Stockport, Cheshire SK1 1TB, tel. 061/480–5799) offers packages to Orlando with a two-center holiday option to Cancun or the Bahamas.

Jetlife Holidays (Suite A, 33 Swanley Centre, Swanley, Kent BR8 7TL, tel. 0322/614801) offers car-inclusive holidays for any duration. There are also tailor-made holidays with the client's own choice of other resorts.

Jetsave Travel Ltd (Sussex House, London, Rd., E. Grinstead, W. Sussex RH19 1LD, tel. 0342/32823) offers several packages to Orlando, with fly/drive and two-center options to other Florida resorts and the Caribbean.

Kuoni Travel (Kuoni House, Dorking, Surrey RH5 4AZ, tel. 0306/740888) has several good packages. They add a rented car for £10 per person to the bargain.

When to Go

Timing is critical; choosing the right time can spell the difference between a good vacation and a great one. On certain days of the year the parks are so packed and the lines so long that you may have time for only a few rides. Then there are many more days when the lines are insignificant.

The first thing to remember is that the busiest days of the week in the Magic Kingdom are Monday, Tuesday, and Wednesday. You would think the weekend would be busiest, but it's not. Perhaps everyone tries to beat the crowds by going in the early part of the week; or perhaps vacationers leave work on Friday,

travel over the weekend, and begin their visits or
Whatever the reason, Friday and Sunday are the slowes___
of the week, and Thursdays and Saturdays are only moderately
busy.

The best times of day to be at the parks are first thing in the
morning (until 11) and in the early and late evening—especially
during summer months and holidays when the attractions stay
open late.

The most crowded time of the year is from Christmas through
New Year's Day. If you hate crowds, avoid this week like the
plague. The parks are also packed around Easter. Memorial
Day weekend is not only crowded, but temperatures can be
quite high. The thought of standing in an hour-long line in humid 90-degree heat should be enough to dissuade you from going then. Other inadvisable times of the year are from mid-June
through mid-August, Thanksgiving weekend, the week of
Washington's Birthday in mid-February, and the weeks of college spring break in late March.

The rest of the year is generally hassle-free, particularly from
early September until just before Thanksgiving. The best time
of all is from just after the Thanksgiving weekend until the beginning of the Christmas holidays. Another excellent time is
from early January through the first week of February. If you
must go during summer, late August is best.

It is a good idea to stay in the most convenient property you can
afford. That way, you can start out bright and early, when the
parks aren't too crowded, go back to your hotel at midday when
they begin to get congested, and return to the parks after dinner, when the crowds will have thinned out considerably.

Climate The following are average daily maximum and minimum temperatures for Orlando.

Jan.	70F	21C	May	88F	31C	Sept.	88F	31C
	49	9		67	19		74	23
Feb.	72F	22C	June	90F	32C	Oct.	83F	28C
	54	12		74	23		67	19
Mar.	76F	24C	July	90F	32C	Nov.	76F	24C
	56	13		74	23		58	14
Apr.	81F	27C	Aug.	90F	32C	Dec.	70F	21C
	63	17		74	23		52	11

Current weather information for more than 750 cities around
the world may be obtained by calling WeatherTrak information
service at 900/370–8728 (cost: 95¢ per minute). A taped message will tell you to dial the three-digit access code for the destination in which you're interested. The code is either the area
code (in the United States) or the first three letters of the foreign city. For a list of all access codes, send a stamped, self-addressed envelope to Cities (9B Terrace Way, Greensboro, NC
27403). For more information, call 800/247–3282.

Festivals and Seasonal Events

Top seasonal events at Disney World and in the Orlando area
include the Florida Citrus Bowl on New Year's Day, the Walt
Disney World Wine Festival in February, Light Up Orlando in
the fall, and the Disney World Halloween and Christmas cele-

brations. For exact dates and further details about the following events, contact the **Orlando/Orange County Convention and Visitors Bureau**, Inc. (8445 International Dr., Orlando, FL 32819, tel. 407/363–5800), or **Walt Disney World** (Box 10040, Lake Buena Vista, FL 32830, tel. 407/824–4321).

Jan. 1: Florida Citrus Bowl Football Classic takes place at Orlando Stadium. Tel. 407/423–2476.

Jan. 4–12: U.S. Figure Skating Championships at Orlando Arena. Tel. 407/784–4249.

Late Jan.: Scottish Highland Games are played at Orlando's Central Florida Fairgrounds. Tel. 407/339–3335.

Early Feb.: Walt Disney World Village Wine Festival includes 60 participating wineries from all over the country. Tel. 407/934–6743.

Late Feb.–early Mar.: Central Florida Fair is held annually at the Central Florida Fairgrounds in Orlando. Tel. 407/295–3247.

Mar.–early Apr.: Houston Astros Spring Training at Osceola County Stadium in Kissimmee. Tel. 407/933–5500.

Mar.–early Apr.: Kansas City Royals Spring Training is at Baseball City Stadium. Tel. 813/424–2424.

Mar. 17: St. Patrick's Day Street Party encourages the wearin' o' the green at Church Street Station. Tel. 407/422–2434.

Mid-Mar.: Nestle Invitational is a regular Professional Golfers Association tour stop at Bay Hill Club in Orlando. Tel. 407/876–2888.

Mid-Mar.: Winter Park Sidewalk Art Festival draws thousands of art enthusiasts to trendy Park Ave. Tel. 407/644–8281.

Easter Sunday: Easter Sunrise Service is presented at the Atlantis Theatre at Sea World, 7007 Sea World Drive, Orlando 32821, tel. 407/351–3600.

Late May: Annual "Up, Up and Away" Airport Art Show takes place at Orlando International Airport. Tel. 407/826–2055.

Late June–Early July: Silver Spurs Rodeo is held in Kissimmee. Tel. 407/847–5000 or 407/847–5118.

Sept.: Oktoberfest includes oompah bands, German folk dancers, German food and beer at Church Street Station. Tel. 407/422–2434.

Mid-Oct.: Walt Disney World PGA Golf Tournament is played on the three Walt Disney World 18-hole golf courses. Tel. 407/824–2250.

Late Oct.: Pioneer Days Folk Festival includes craftspeople and musicians at the Center Grounds on Randolph Street in Pine Castle. Tel. 407/855–7461.

Oct. 31: Halloween Street Party is held at Church Street Station. Tel. 407/422–2434.

Mid-Nov.: Festival of the Masters is an art festival with works by 230 top artists held at Walt Disney World Village. Tel. 407/934–6743.

Mid-Nov.: Light Up Orlando is a street party downtown with live entertainment. Tel. 407/648–4010.

Early Dec.: Pet Fair & Winterfest is held in Orlando's Loch Haven Park. Tel. 407/644–2739.

Early Dec.: Annual Half Marathon begins in Lake Eola Park in downtown Orlando. Tel. 407/898–1313.

Dec.: Glory and Pageantry of Christmas Nativity Scene is at Walt Disney World Village. Tel. 407/934–6743.

Dec. 31: Citrus Bowl Parade takes place in Orlando. Tel. 407/629–4944.

What to Pack

Winters are mild in Orlando and summers are hot and humid. Daytime temperatures in the winter months average in the 70s and low 80s, but evening temperatures can dip to the 60s, so take a sweater or jacket, just in case. Year round, be prepared for air-conditioning bordering on the glacial. Orlando and Disney World are extremely casual, day and night. Men will need a jacket and tie for only a handful of restaurants. Casual resort wear is the norm elsewhere. For sightseeing and visits to Disney World, pack walking shorts, sundresses, cotton slacks, and T-shirts. Comfortable walking shoes or sneakers are essential. Pack an umbrella for sudden thunderstorms during the summer, but leave the plastic raincoats behind; they're extremely uncomfortable in the high humidity. In the summer, you'll want a sun hat and plenty of sunscreen lotion, even for strolls in the city, because the sun can be fierce.

Cash Machines

Virtually all U.S. banks belong to a network of ATMs (Automatic Teller Machines) that dispense cash 24 hours a day in cities throughout the country. There are some eight major networks in the USA, the largest of which are Cirrus, owned by MasterCard, and Plus, affiliated with Visa. Some banks belong to more than one network. These cards are not automatically issued; you have to apply for them. Cards issued by Visa and MasterCard also may be used in the ATMs, but the fees are usually higher than the fees on bank cards. There is also a daily interest charge on credit card "loans," even if monthly bills are paid on time. Each network has a toll-free number you can call to locate machines in a given city. The Cirrus number is 800/4–CIRRUS; the Plus number is 800/THE–PLUS. Check with your bank for information on fees and on the amount of cash you can withdraw on any given day. Express Cash allows American Express cardholders to withdraw up to $1,000 in a seven day period (21 days overseas) from their personal checking accounts at ATMs worldwide. Gold cardmembers can receive up to $2,500 in a seven day period (21 days overseas). Express Cash is not a cash advance service; only money already in the linked checking account can be withdrawn. Every transaction carries a 2% fee with a minimum charge of $2 and a maximum of $6. Apply for a PIN (Personal Identification number) and to link your accounts at least 2–3 weeks before departure. Call 800/CASH–NOW to receive an application or to locate the nearest Express Cash machine.

Traveling with Film

If your camera is new, shoot and develop a few rolls before leaving home. Pack some lens tissue and an extra battery for your built-in light meter. Invest about $10 in a skylight filter and screw it onto the front of your lens. It will protect the lens and also reduce haze.

Film doesn't like hot weather. If you're driving in summer, don't store film in the glove compartment or on the shelf under the rear window. Put it behind the front seat on the floor, on the side opposite the exhaust pipe.

On a plane trip, never pack unprocessed film in check-in luggage; if your bags get X-rayed, you can say goodbye to your pictures. Always carry undeveloped film with you through security and ask to have it inspected by hand. (It helps to isolate your film in a plastic bag, ready for quick inspection.) Inspectors at American airports are required by law to honor requests for hand inspection; abroad, you'll have to depend on the kindness of strangers.

The old airport scanning machines—still in use in some Third World countries—use heavy doses of radiation that can turn a family portrait into an early morning fog. The newer models—used in all U.S. airports—are safe for anything from five to 500 scans, depending on the speed of your film. The effects are cumulative; you can put the same roll of film through several scans without worry. After five scans, though, you're asking for trouble.

If your film gets fogged and you want an explanation, send it to the **National Association of Photographic Manufacturers, Inc.** (550 Mamaroneck Ave., Harrison, NY 10528, tel. 914/698-7603). They will try to determine what went wrong. The service is free.

Car Rentals

It is by no means absolutely necessary to rent a car when you are in Orlando. Just about every hotel, and even many motels, are linked to one of several private transportation systems that shuttle travelers back and forth to most of the area attractions for only a few dollars. And if you are staying at a Disney hotel or purchase a Passport (4 or more days) instead of daily tickets, your transportation within Disney World is free.

Should you want to visit some of the less frequented attractions outside of Disney World, however, or dine in restaurants that are off the beaten tourist track, then a rental car is essential. Keep in mind that public transportation in Orlando is practically nonexistent. As for taxi cabs, try not to think about them unless you're going a short distance. Everything in Orlando is spread out and hopping in a cab every time you want to go someplace may put you on an expressway to the poorhouse.

Fortunately, Orlando offers some of the lowest rental car rates in the entire United States—not what you would expect from one of the tourist capitals of the world. The secret is to rent at special weekly rates and not return the car before the week is up. If you keep a car less than seven days, be prepared to pay daily rates—which can cost twice as much as weekly rates. It's the sort of promotional gimmickry for which car rentals companies are infamous.

When renting, be sure to consider taking out Collision Damage Waiver (CDW) insurance. It costs a few dollars more but is usually worth it, because even the smallest fender-bender can be outrageously expensive. Your own car insurance policy may cover rentals, but you will have to advance the cost of damage until the claim is settled, which can deplete your supply of cash or exceed the limit on your credit card.

Many car rental companies have counters in the major hotels and on Level 2 of the Orlando airport. Companies with offices in Orlando or near, but not actually in, the airport, have rates

that are generally lower. These budget firms usually have free
pickup service at the hotels and the airport.

Orlando **Alamo** (tel. 800/327–9633). # 6935837
International **Avis** (tel. 800/331–1212).
Airport **Budget** (tel. 800/527–0700).
Dollar (tel. 800/800–4000).
Hertz (tel. 800/654–3131).
National (tel. 800/328–4567).
Superior (tel. 800/237–8106; 407/857–2023 in FL.).
Thrifty (tel. 800/367–2277).

Traveling with Children

All hotels on Disney property have playgrounds and game
rooms with pinball machines and video games. The Contemporary, Dolphin, Grand Floridian, Polynesian Village, and Swan
each has child-care facilities. All guests in the Orlando area can
make use of the preschool and day-care facilities at Walt Disney
World. *Children from 6 months to 12 years are accepted Mon.–
Sat., 6 AM–10 PM and Sun., 6 AM–9 PM. Tel. 407/827–KIDS.*

If you're worried about your children getting lost, get them
name tags either at the Magic Kingdom (at City Hall or at the
Baby Center next to the Crystal Palace), at Epcot Center (at
Earth Station or the Baby Care Center), or at Disney-MGM
Studios Theme Park (at Guest Services).

If your children do get lost, check the lost children's logbooks in
either the Baby Care Center or City Hall in the Magic Kingdom; in either the Earth Station or the Baby Care Center behind the Odyssey Restaurant in Epcot Center; or at Guest
Services at Disney-MGM.

Strollers may be rented at the stroller shop near the entrance
to the Magic Kingdom (on the east side of Main St.); at the
French pavilion or at the stroller shop (east of entrance) at
Epcot; or at Oscar's at Disney-MGM.

All three Disney parks have Baby Care Centers with facilities
for changing infants and preparing formulas. Baby food, pacifi-
ers, and disposable diapers can be purchased here. Travelers
not staying on Disney property can make baby-sitting arrange-
ments with the hotel concierge or housekeeper, or by contact-
ing **Fairy Godmother's Child Care** (tel. 407/277–3724).

Breakfasts Kids love these daily breakfasts, where they can hold hands
with and give bear hugs to all the best-loved Disney characters—Mickey, Minnie, Goofy, Donald, and others. Mickey and
his friends appear each morning at the Empress Lilly and at
the Contemporary Resort Hotel Cafe. Mary Poppins and her
friends have breakfast at the café at the Grand Floridian Beach
Resort. Disney characters also drop in Sundays at the Water-
cress Café at the Buena Vista Palace at Walt Disney World Village. Prices and times may vary, so call ahead. **Empress Lilly:**
*tel. 407/828–3900. Reservations required. Serving 8:30–10 AM.
Cost: $9.95 adults, $6.50 children 3–11.* **Contemporary:** *tel.
407/934–7639. Reservations not required. Serving 8–11 AM.
Cost: $9.95 adults, $5.95 children 3–11.* **Grand Floridian:** *tel.
407/824–2383. Reservations accepted. Serving 7:30 AM–noon.
Cost: $13.25 adults, $8.75 children 3–11.* **Buena Vista Palace:**
*tel. 407/827–2727. Serving 8–10:30 AM. Cost: $11.95 adults,
$6.95 children under 11.*

Brunch The Disney characters have Sunday brunch at the Ristorante Carnivale at the Dolphin. *Tel. 407/934–6165. Reservations advised. Serving 9 AM–1 PM. Cost: $15.95 adults; $7.95 children 4–11.*

Dinner Mickey's Tropical Revue is a luau character show at the Papeete Bay Verandah. Chip and Dale, dressed as the Rescue Rangers, are at the buffet at the Grand Floridian's 1900 Park Fare Restaurant. **Polynesian Resort:** *tel. 407/W–DISNEY. Reservations required. Serving at 4:30 PM. Cost: $25 adults, $20 patrons 12–20, $11 children. No smoking.* **Grand Floridian:** *tel. 407/824–3000. No reservations. Serving 5–9 PM. Cost: $17.50 adults, $8.50 children 3–11.* **Chef Mickey's Village Restaurant:** *tel. 407/828–3723. Reservations advised. Serving 5:30–10 PM. Cost: entrees $10.25–$17.95; children's menu entrees $3.25–$6.50.*

Lodging In all but the smallest motels there is little or no charge for children under 18 who share a room with an adult.

Publications *Family Travel Times* is an 8- to 12-page newsletter published 10 times a year by TWYCH (Travel with Your Children, 80 Eighth Ave., New York, NY 10011, tel. 212/206–0688). A subscription, which costs $35 a year, includes access to back issues and twice-weekly opportunities to phone for specific advice.

Getting There On domestic flights, children under 2 not occupying a seat travel free. Various discounts apply to children 2–12. Reserve a seat behind the bulkhead of the plane, which offers more leg room and can usually fit a bassinet (supplied by the airline). At the same time, inquire about special children's meals or snacks, offered by most airlines. (See "TWYCH's Airline Guide" in the February 1990 and 1992 issues of *Family Travel Times* for a rundown on the services offered by 46 different airlines.) Ask in advance if you can bring aboard your child's car seat. For the booklet "Child/Infant Safety Seats Acceptable for Use in Aircraft," write Community and Consumer Liaison Division, APA–200 Federal Aviation Administration, Washington, DC 20591, tel. 202/267–3479.

Hints for Older Travelers

The American Association of Retired Persons (AARP, 1909 K St., NW, Washington, DC 20049, tel. 202/662–4850) has two programs for independent travelers: (1) *The Purchase Privilege Program,* which offers discounts on hotels, airfare (American Airlines only), car rentals, RV rentals, and sightseeing; and (2) the *AARP Motoring Plan,* provided by Amoco, which offers emergency aid and trip routing information for an annual fee of $33.95 per couple. AARP members must be 50 or older. Annual AARP dues are $5 per person or per couple.

When using an AARP or other identification card, ask for a reduced hotel rate when you make your reservation, not when you check out. At participating restaurants, show your card to the maitre d' before you are seated, since discounts may be limited to certain set menus, days, or hours. When renting a car, be sure to ask about special promotional rates that might offer greater savings than the available discount.

Travel Industry and Disabled Exchange (TIDE, 5435 Donna Ave., Tarzana, CA 91356, tel. 818/368–5648) is an industry-based organization with a $15 per person annual membership fee. Members receive a quarterly newsletter and a directory of travel agencies that serve the disabled.

National Council of Senior Citizens (925 15th St., NW, Washington, DC 20005, tel. 202/347–8800) is a nonprofit advocacy group with some 5,000 local clubs across the country. Annual membership is $12 single or per couple, one year; $30 per person, three years; $150 per person, lifetime. Members receive a monthly newspaper with travel information and an ID card for reduced rates on hotels and car rentals.

Saga International Holidays (120 Boylston St., Boston, MA 02116, tel. 800/343–0273) specializes in group travel for people over 60. A selection of variously priced tours allows you to choose the package that meets your needs.

Mature Outlook (6001 N. Clark St., Chicago, IL 60660, tel. 800/336–6330), a subsidiary of Sears Roebuck & Co., is a travel club for people over 50, with hotel and motel discounts and a bimonthly newsletter. Annual membership is $9.95 per couple. Membership applications are available at Sears stores and participating Holiday Inns.

Golden Age Passport is a free lifetime pass to all parks, monuments, and recreation areas run by the federal government. People over 62 should pick them up in person at any national park that charges admission. A driver's license or other proof of age is required.

September Days Club is run by the moderately priced Days Inns of America (tel. 800/241–5050). The $12 annual membership fee for individuals or couples over 50 entitles them to reduced car rental rates and reductions of 15–50% at some 95% of the chain's motels.

Greyhound (tel. 800/752–4841) and **Amtrak** (tel. 800/USA–RAIL) offer special fares for senior citizens. Amtrak has a free access guide.

The Senior Citizen's Guide to Budget Travel in the United States and Canada is available for $3.95, plus $1 for shipping, from Pilot Books (103 Cooper St., Babylon, NY 11702, tel. 516/422–2225).

The Discount Guide for Travelers over 55, by Caroline and Walter Weintz, lists helpful addresses, package tours, reduced-rate car rentals, etc., in the USA and abroad. It is available for $7.95, plus $1.50 shipping, from Penguin USA/NAL (Bergenfield Order Dept., 120 Woodbine St., Bergenfield, NJ 07621, tel. 800/526–0275). Include ISBN 0–525–483–58–6 in your order.

Hints for Disabled Travelers

A free booklet, "The Disabled Guest," is available from Disney World by calling 407/824–4321. Facilities are extensive, including wheelchair rentals near the entrances to the Magic Kingdom, Epcot, and MGM.

The Information Center for Individuals with Disabilities (Fort Point Pl., 1st floor, 27–43 Wormwood St., Boston, MA 02210, tel. 617/727–5540; TDD 617/727–5236) offers useful problem-solving assistance, including lists of travel agents that specialize in tours for the disabled.

Moss Rehabilitation Hospital Travel Information Service; Philadelphia, PA 19141, tel. 215/456–9600; TDD 215/456–9602) provides information on tourist sights, transportation, and accommodations in destinations around the world.

Mobility International USA (Box 3551, Eugene, OR 97403, tel. 503/343-1284) has information on accommodations, organized study, etc., around the world.

The Society for the Advancement of Travel for the Handicapped (26 Court St., Brooklyn, NY 11242, tel. 718/858-5483) offers access information. Annual membership costs $45, or $25 for senior travelers and students. Send a stamped, self-addressed envelope.

Greyhound (tel. 800/752-4841) will carry a disabled person and companion for the price of a single fare. **Amtrak** (tel. 800/USA-RAIL) requests advance notice to provide redcap service, special seats, and a 25% discount.

The Itinerary (Box 2012, Bayonne, NJ 07002, tel. 201/858-3400) is a bimonthly travel magazine for the disabled.

Access to the World: A Travel Guide for the Handicapped by Louise Weiss is available from Henry Holt & Co. (Box 30135, Salt Lake City, UT 84130 (tel. 800/247-3912), for $12.95 plus $2 shipping; include order number 0805001417).

Further Reading

Still the most perceptive book on Disney is *The Disney Version* (1985 edition) by Richard Schickel. Disney's art is featured in *Disneyland: Inside Story*, by Randy Bright, a $35 art book published by Harry N. Abrams. Much of the action in Tom Wolfe's *The Right Stuff* (1984) takes place at Cape Canaveral, near Orlando. For a good read about Disney and other animators, look for *Of Mice and Magic* (1987) by Leonard Maltin. *Walt Disney: An American Original* (1976) by Bob Thomas is full of anecdotes about the development of WDW.

Arriving and Departing

By Plane

More than 21 scheduled airlines and more than 30 charters operate in and out of Orlando International Airport, with direct service to more than 100 U.S. cities as well as to major cities in Europe, South America, Canada, and most recently Asia. At last count, Delta, the official airline of Disney World, had 70 flights daily to and from Orlando. Travel packages to Disney World are offered by Delta (tel. 800/872-7786). When booking reservations, keep in mind the distinction between nonstop flights (no stops and no changes), direct flights (no changes of aircraft, but one or more stops), and connecting flights (one or more changes of planes at one or more stops). Connecting flights are often the least expensive, but they are the most time-consuming, and the biggest nuisance.

Major U.S. airlines that serve Orlando include American, Bahamasair, British Airways, Continental, Delta, Icelandair, KLM, Mexicana, Midway, Northwest, Pan Am, TransBrasil, TWA, United, and USAir.

The Orlando airport has a Disney World information booth where tickets, maps, and information are available. Buying tickets here while waiting for your bags to be off-loaded will save time later on.

Smoking As of late February 1990, smoking was banned on all routes within the 48 contiguous states; within the states of Hawaii and Alaska; to and from the U.S. Virgin Islands and Puerto Rico; and on flights of under six hours to and from Hawaii and Alaska. The rule applies to both U.S. and foreign carriers.

On a flight where smoking is permitted, you can request a nonsmoking seat during check-in or when you book your ticket. If the airline tells you there are no seats available in the nonsmoking section on the day of the flight, insist on one: Department of Transportation regulations require carriers to find seats for all nonsmokers, provided they meet check-in time restrictions. These regulations apply to all international flights on U.S. carriers; however, the Department of Transportation does not have jurisdiction over foreign carriers traveling out of, or into, the United States.

Carry-on Luggage Under new rules in effect since January 1988, passengers are usually limited to two carry-on bags. For bags stored under your seat, the maximum dimensions are 9″ × 14″ × 22″, a total of 45″. For bags that can be hung in a closet, the maximum dimensions are 4″ × 23″ × 45″, a total of 72″. For bags stored in an overhead bin, the maximum dimensions are 10″ × 14″ × 36″, a total of 60″. Any item that exceeds the specified dimensions will generally be rejected as a carryon, and handled as checked baggage. Keep in mind that an airline can adapt these rules to circumstances, so on an especially crowded flight don't be surprised if you are allowed only one carry-on bag.

In addition to the two bags, passengers may also carry aboard: a handbag (pocketbook or purse), an overcoat or wrap, an umbrella, a camera, a reasonable amount of reading material, an infant bag, and crutches, a cane, braces, or other prosthetic devices upon which the passenger is dependent. Infant/child safety seats also be brought aboard if parents have purchased a ticket for the child or if there is space in the cabin.

Note that these regulations are for U.S. airlines only. Foreign airlines generally allow one piece of carry-on luggage in tourist class, in addition to handbags and bags filled with duty-free goods. Passengers in first and business class also may be allowed to carry on one garment bag. It is best to check with your airline ahead of time to find out what its exact rules are regarding carry-on luggage.

Certain toy guns, toy knives, etc., sold in Frontierland and Adventureland should be packed in checked luggage. Security may give you a hard time if you try to carry them on board.

Checked Luggage U.S. airlines generally allow passengers to check in two suitcases whose total dimensions (length + width + height) do not exceed 62″ and whose weight (per piece) does not exceed 70 pounds.

Rules governing foreign airlines vary from airline to airline, so check with your travel agent or the airline itself before you go. All the airlines allow passengers to check in two bags. In general, expect the weight restriction on the two bags to be not more than 70 lbs. each, and the size restriction to be not more than 62″ total dimensions per bag.

Lost Luggage On domestic flights, airlines are responsible for lost or damaged property only up to $1,250 per passenger. If you're carrying valuables, either take them with you on the airplane or purchase additional insurance for lost luggage. Some airlines will issue additional luggage insurance when you check in, but many do not. Insurance for lost, damaged, or stolen luggage is available through travel agents or directly through various insurance companies. Two that issue luggage insurance are **Tele-Trip** (Box 31685, 3201 Farnam St., Omaha, NE 68131, tel. 800/228–9792), a subsidiary of Mutual of Omaha, and **The Travelers Corporation** (Ticket and Travel Dept., 1 Tower Sq., Hartford, CT 06183, tel. 203/277–0111 or 800/243–3174). Tele-Trip operates sales booths at airports, and also issues insurance through travel agents. Tele-Trip will insure checked or hand luggage through its travel insurance packages. Rates vary according to the length of the trip. The Travelers Corporation will insure checked or hand luggage from $500 to $2,000 valuation per person, for a maximum of 180 days. Rates for 1–5 days for $500 valuation are $10; for 180 days, $85.

Other companies with comprehensive policies include **Access America Inc.,** a subsidiary of Blue Cross-Blue Shield (Box 11188, Richmond, VA 23230, tel. 800/334–7525) and **Near Services** (450 Prairie Ave., Suite 101, Calumet City, IL 60409, tel. 708/868–6700 or 800/654–6700).

Before you go, itemize the contents of each bag in case you need to file an insurance claim. Be certain to put your home address on each piece of luggage, including carry-on bags. If your luggage is stolen and later recovered, the airline will deliver the luggage to your home free of charge.

Between the Airport and the Hotels There are several shuttle and limousine services at the airport that offer regularly scheduled service (as well as charter service) to and from many major hotels, leaving every half-hour to Disney properties and every hour to less busy destinations. Ticket counters are in the baggage claim area. When making hotel reservations, check to see if your hotel offers free shuttle service from the airport. If not, ask for the name of the service that is most convenient.

By Bus You can catch a public bus between the airport and downtown Orlando, which goes to and from the main terminal of the **Tri-County Transit Authority** (1200 W. South St., Orlando, tel. 407/841–8240). The cost is 75¢ and a dime for a transfer. The downtown area, however, is far from most hotels, so you might want to consider other options.

By Limousine **Mears Transportation Group** (tel. 407/423–5566) sends 11-passenger vans to Disney World and along Rte. 192 every 30 minutes. Prices begin at $13 one way for adults, $8 for children 4–11; to $22 round-trip adults, $12 children 4–11. **Town & Country Limo** (tel. 407/828–3035) and **First Class Transportation** (tel. 407/578–0022) also offer limousine service.

By Taxi Taxis are the fastest way to get from the airport to wherever you will be staying (25–30 minutes at most), but the ride won't be cheap. To Walt Disney World hotels or to hotels along U.S. 192 W, a cab trip will cost about $35 plus tip. To the International Drive area, it will cost about $25 plus tip. Cabs queue at the airport.

By Car When you leave the airport, catch the Beeline Expressway (Rte. 528) west to International Drive and exit at Sea World. Or stay on the Beeline to I–4, and head either west to Disney

World or east to downtown Orlando. You would be wise to call your hotel for the best route.

By Car

If you want to have your car in Florida without having to drive it there, put it aboard the **Auto-Train** in Lorton, VA, near Washington, DC. The train goes to Sanford, FL, some 23 miles from Orlando.

By Train

Amtrak (tel. 800/USA–RAIL) stops in Winter Park (150 Morse Blvd.), in Orlando (1400 Sligh Blvd.), and then, 20 minutes later, in Kissimmee (416 Pleasant St.).

By Bus

Contact **Greyhound** (555 N. Magruder Ave., Orlando, tel. 407/843–7720) or consult your phone book or directory assistance for a local number that will automatically connect you with the national Greyhound Information Center.

Staying in Orlando

Important Addresses and Numbers

Tourist Information For **Walt Disney World** information and brochures, go to any ticket window or call 407/824–4321 daily 8 AM–9 PM.

The **Visitor Information Center** (8445 International Dr., in the Mercado Mediterranean Village, tel. 407/363–5800) is the main information office for the Orlando area.

Kissimmee–St. Cloud Tourist Information (1925 E. Irlo Bronson Memorial Hwy., tel. 407/847–5000, Kissimmee; 407/423–6070, Orlando) is 2½ miles east of I–4 on Rte. 192.

For accommodations call the 24-hour, free **Central Reservation Service** (800/950–0232).

Emergencies **Police** or **Ambulance,** tel. 911.

Doctors Hospital emergency rooms are open 24 hours a day. The most accessible hospital, located in the International Dr. area, is the **Orlando Regional Medical Center/Sand Lake Hospital** (9400 Turkey Lake Rd., tel. 407/351–8500).

For hotel-room visits by physicians for minor medical care and non-narcotic medicine, contact a mobile minor emergency service called **Housemed** (tel. 407/648–9234 and 407/846–2093 in Kissimmee).

For minor medical problems, visit the **Family Treatment Center** (6001 Vineland Rd., one block west of Kirkman Rd., tel. 407/351–6682).

If you are staying near Lake Buena Vista, a convenient new facility is the **Buena Vista Walk-in Medical Center** (adjacent to the Walt Disney World Village entrance on S.R. 535, tel. 407/828–3434). It's open daily 9–8. Shuttle service is available from any of Disney's first-aid stations for $15 round-trip.

24-Hour Pharmacies **Eckerd Drugs** (908 Lee Rd., Orlando, tel. 407/644–6908).

Walgreen Drug Store (2410 E. Colonial Dr., Orlando, tel. 407/894–6781).

Dentists **Emergency dental referral,** tel. 407/847–7474.

Road Service **AAA Emergency Road Service,** tel. 407/877–2266 or 800/824–4432.

24-Hour Market **Gooding's Supermarket** (7600 Dr. Phillips Blvd., tel. 407/352–8851) is conveniently located off I–4, a few blocks from International Drive.

Gooding's Supermarket (12521 S.R. 535, tel. 827–1200) is at the Crossroads of Lake Buena Vista at Exit 27 of I–4.

Disney World Walt Disney World Information, tel. 407/824–4321.

Accommodations Reservations, tel. 407/W–DISNEY.

Dinner Show Reservations, tel. 407/W–DISNEY.

WDW Resort Dining/Recreation Information, tel. 407/824–3737.

Tours (Magic Kingdom & Epcot Center), tel. 407/824–4321.

Walt Disney World Resort Lost & Found, tel. 407/824–4245.

Magic Kingdom Lost & Found, tel. 407/824–4521.

Epcot Center Lost & Found, tel. 407/560–6105.

Disney-MGM Studios Theme Park Lost & Found, tel. 407/420–4668.

Car Care Center, tel. 407/824–4813.

Western Union at WDW, tel. 407/824–3456.

Banking Information (Sun Bank), tel. 407/824–5767.

Time and Weather, tel. 407/422–1611.

Walt Disney World Shopping Village Information, tel. 407/828–3058.

KinderCare Child Care, tel. 407/827–5444, private, or 407/827–5437, group.

Getting Around

By Car The most important artery in the Orlando area is **Interstate 4 (I–4).** This interstate ties everything together, and you'll invariably receive directions in reference to it. The problem is that I–4 is considered an east-west expressway in our national road system (the even numbers refer to an east-west orientation, the odd numbers to a north-south orientation). I–4 does run from east to west *if* you follow it from the Atlantic Coast to Florida's Gulf of Mexico. But in the Orlando area I–4 actually runs north and south. Always remember, therefore, that when the signs say east you are often going north, and when the signs say west, you are often going south. Think north-EAST and south-WEST.

Another main drag is **International Drive,** which has several major hotels, restaurants, and shopping centers. You can get onto International Drive from I–4 exits 28, 29, and 30B.

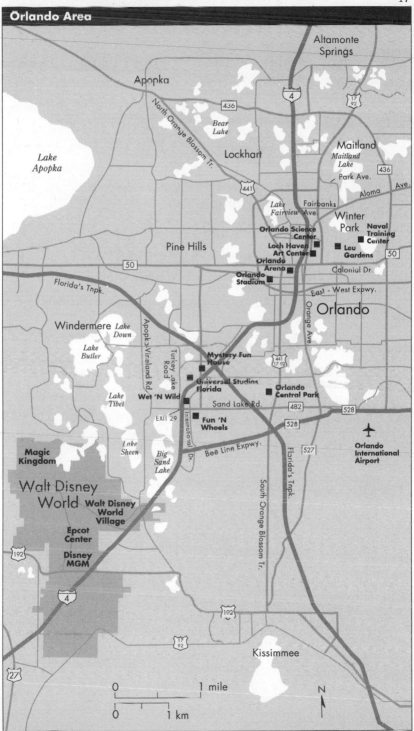

Orlando Area

Altamonte Springs

Apopka

436

4

17 92

Lake Apopka

Bear Lake

Lockhart

Maitland

Maitland Lake

436

Park Ave.

441

Aloma Ave.

Lake Fairview

Fairbanks Ave.

Winter Park

Naval Training Center

Pine Hills

Orlando Science Center

Loch Haven Art Center

Leu Gardens

50

Orlando Arena

Colonial Dr.

50

Orlando Stadium

East - West Expwy.

Florida's Tnpk.

Orlando

Orange Ave.

Windermere

Lake Down

Lake Butler

Apopka-Vineland Rd.

Turkey Lake Road

Mystery Fun House

441 17 92

Lake Tibet

Wet 'N Wild

Universal Studios Florida

Orlando Central Park

Sand Lake Rd.

482

528

EXIT 29

International Dr.

Fun 'N Wheels

528

527

Lake Sheen

Big Sand Lake

Bee Line Expwy.

Orlando International Airport

Magic Kingdom

South Orange Blossom Tr.

Florida's Tnpk.

Walt Disney World

Walt Disney World Village

Epcot Center

192

Disney MGM

4

192

27

17 92

Kissimmee

0   1 mile

0   1 km

N

The other main road, **U.S. 192,** cuts across I–4 at exits 25A and 25B. This highway goes through the Kissimmee area and crosses Walt Disney World property, taking you to the Magic Kingdom's main entrance. U.S. 192 may sometimes be called by one of its former names, Spacecoast Parkway or Irlo Bronson Memorial Highway.

By Bus If you are staying along International Drive, in Kissimmee, or in Orlando proper, you can take advantage of the limited public bus system, but only to get places within the immediate area. To find out which bus to take, ask your hotel clerk or call the **Tri-County Transit Authority Information Office** (tel. 407/841–8240) during business hours. A transfer will add 10¢ to the regular 75¢ fare.

By Taxi Taxi fares start at $2.45 and cost $1.30 for each mile thereafter. Call **Yellow Cab Co.** (tel. 407/699–9999) or **Town and Country Cab** (tel. 407/828–3035).

From the Hotels to the Attractions There are many transportation services available serving just about every hotel and major attraction in the area. Many offer both scheduled service and charters. All hotels can arrange pickups and drop-offs to and from attractions. Transportation usually costs less than $5 each way. For attractions such as Busch Gardens and Cypress Gardens, which are more than a half-hour's drive, expect to pay a single price of about $27 per person, which includes round-trip fare and admission. Different services schedule these trips on different days of the week. Call in advance for reservations. Companies offering both scheduled and charter transportation include **Gray Line of Orlando** (tel. 407/422–0744), **Rabbit Bus Lines** (tel. 407/291–2424), and **Phoenix Tours** (tel. 407/859–4211).

Guided Tours

Walt Disney World A good way to get a feel for the layout of the Magic Kingdom, along with some interesting commentary about what goes on behind the scenes and inside tips on how to see the attractions in the most efficient way, is to take one of the guided orientation tours.

These 3½- to 4-hour tours cost $5 per adult and $3.50 per child, in addition to admission price. Tours include visits to some of the rides and pavilions, but don't expect to go to the head of the line. This is not like taking ski lessons; you still have to wait your turn even though you're with an official tour guide.

To find out the schedule, ask at the information desk in City Hall in the Magic Kingdom, or at the guided tour booth at the Epcot entrance plaza, tel. 407/824–4321.

Helicopter Rides **Falcon Helicopter Service, Inc.,** tours over Orlando's attractions. *8990 International Dr. (next to King Henry's Feast), Orlando, tel. 407/352–1753, or at the Hyatt Hotel at I–4 and U.S. 192, Kissimmee, tel. 407/396–7222. Cost: $35–$98 adults, $20–$50 children.*

Ballooning **Balloon Flights of Florida.** This Church Street Station event is not cheap, but it's an experience you'll never forget. The flight, flown by a balloonist who made the first trip across the Atlantic, is followed by brunch at Lili Marlene's, *124 W. Pine St., Orlando, tel. 407/841–UPUP. Cost: $150 per person.*

Rise & Float Balloon Tours. Two of the most popular flights are the Champagne Balloon Excursion, which provides a bird's-eye view of all major attractions, *(Cost: $150 single, $280 couples, $75 children under 11)* and the romantic For Lovers Only ($350 per couple), which includes champagne, fruits, cheeses, crackers, and pastries. Rise & Float's newest addition is a 210,000-cubic-foot hot-air balloon (about the size of a Goodyear Blimp) embellished with two hot pink flamingos and a giant palm tree. *5767 Major Blvd. (at the Mystery Fun House), Orlando, tel. 407/352–8191.*

2 Portrait o. Walt Disney

The Disney Version

by Richard Schickel

Mr. Schickel has reviewed movies for Time *since 1972. Before that he was film critic for* Life. *His many books include* The Disney Version *and* Intimate Strangers: The Culture of Celebrity.

Among unsophisticated people there was a common misapprehension that Disney continued to draw at least the important sequences in his animated films, his comic strips, his illustrated books. Although his studio often stressed in its publicity the numbers of people it employed and the beauties of their teamwork, some *very* unsophisticated people thought he did everything himself—an interesting example of the persistence of a particularly treasured illusion and of the corporation's ability to keep it alive even while denying it.

Disney himself once tried to explain his role in his company by telling a story that may well be apocryphal but is no less significant and no less quoted in company publicity for all that. "You know," he said, "I was stumped one day when a little boy asked, 'Do you draw Mickey Mouse?' I had to admit I did not draw any more. 'Then you think up all the jokes and ideas?' 'No,' I said, 'I don't do that.' Finally he looked at me and said, 'Mr. Disney, just what do you do?'

"'Well,' I said, 'sometimes I think of myself as a little bee. I go from one area of the studio to another and gather pollen and sort of stimulate everybody.' I guess that's the job I do."

The summary is not a bad one, as far as it goes. But there were a good many more wrinkles in Disney's situation than the smoothness of this explanation would indicate. For one thing, Disney was continually, if mildly, irked because he could not draw Mickey or Donald or Pluto. He never could. Even Mickey Mouse was designed by someone else, namely Ub Iwerks, an old friend from Disney's pre-Hollywood days. Iwerks actually received screen credit for so doing on the first Mouse cartoons. In later years Disney was known to apply to his animators for hints on how to render a quick sketch of Mickey in order to oblige autograph hunters who requested it to accompany his signature. Even more embarrassingly, he could not accurately duplicate the familiar "Walt Disney" signature that appeared as a trademark on all his products. There are people who received authentically autographed Disney books and records but who thought they were fake because his hand did not match that of the trademark—a particular irony in the case of Disney, who had devoted a lifetime to publicizing his name and, as we have seen, quite literally capitalizing on it.

Stories like these should not be taken to mean that Disney passed his final years living out the myth that money cannot

Reprinted from The Disney Version *(Touchstone, 1968) by permission of the author.*

buy happiness or that when his fortune caught up with his fame he found that all his dreams were a mockery. Far from it. Like many men who have grown rich through their own efforts, he had little use for personal display. His suits were still bought off the peg. His diet still consisted largely of the foods he had acquired a taste for in the hash houses of his youth (hamburgers, steaks and chops were staples; he especially liked chili). He drove himself to work, mostly in standard American cars, though in his last year he took to using the Jaguar that Roddy MacDowall had driven in *That Darned Cat*. He served tomato juice to visitors in his office but allowed beer to be served in the studio commissary—by no means a standard Hollywood practice—and admitted to enjoying a highball or two at the end of a workday that minimally ran twelve hours.

He traveled mainly on business and submitted to vacations with restless grouchiness. His one known extravagance was the scale model train that used to circle his home and that he conceived and then helped to build. In the early Fifties it had been his great pleasure to don a railroad engineer's cap, brandish a slender-spouted railroader's oilcan and pilot grandchildren and other visitors around his yard.

The train became, over the years, the subject of a disproportionate share of Disney lore. It was as if he used it to distract attention from other areas of his private life—certainly it made excellent feature copy for popular journalism. Mrs. Disney and his daughters tried to persuade him to build the thing at the studio instead of in his yard, but he went so far as to have his lawyers draft a right-of-way contract for his family to sign giving him permission to build and maintain the train. It was a token of such seriousness of intent that they agreed to sign it, whereupon he declared that in the circumstances their verbal consent was good enough for him. He loved fussing over the train, continually adding to its supply of rolling stock, improving the grades, even digging a tunnel so that it could pass under some of his wife's flower gardens without disturbing them. Mrs. Disney once commented, "It is a wonderful hobby for him . . . it has been a fine diversion and safety valve for his nervous energy. For when he leaves the studio he can't just lock the door and forget it. He is so keyed up he has to keep going on something."

She noted that a good deal of their social life in this period revolved around giving people rides on the half-mile line and that a select few were given cards designating them vice presidents of the road. She and her daughters quickly became bored with the train, but Disney did not, and he even suffered some hurt feelings over their indifference. He enjoyed—like a small boy with an electric train—planning wrecks because repairing the damage was so much fun. Once, after he bought two new engines, she heard him enthusing to George Murphy, the former Senator and then one of the toy train line's "vice presidents," "Boy, we're sure to have some wrecks now!"

The train was the only splash of color in the Disneys' quiet home life. Their friends, with the exception of Murphy, Kay Kayser, Irene Dunne and a few others, were not drawn from show business. Indeed, their daughter, Diane, became the first daughter of a motion-picture-industry family to make her debut at the Las Madrinas Ball in Los Angeles (which, in 1967, finally invited its first Jewish girl to participate). To old Angelenos the movies and the Jews were, apparently, virtually synonymous. Of the other aspects of Disney's mature home life little is known. He is recorded as having been a doting father, given to sentimental outbursts on such occasions as weddings and the birth of grandchildren, and the indulgent master of a poodle, for whom he was known to raid the ice box for cold meat. He also forbade the extermination of small pests—rabbits, squirrels and the like—that raided his wife's garden. This was, so far as one can tell, no idle image-protection on his part, but rather an expression of genuine concern for animal life. Outside the home his favorite recreation was wandering around— unrecognized, he hoped—in such places as the Farmer's Market in Los Angeles or on New York's Third Avenue, where he liked to browse the secondhand and antique shops and buy dollhouse-sized furniture. He had, Mrs. Disney reported, "no use for people who throw their weight around as celebrities, or for those who fawn over you just because you are famous."

Among countless perquisites that were available to him as the head of a prospering corporation, the only one that seemed to afford him much pleasure was the company's three-plane "airline," the flagship of which was a prop-jet Grumman Gulfstream. He went everywhere on it and took an open—perhaps even childlike— pride in this particular symbolization of his status. In the months before he died, he frequently mentioned the pure jet that Walt Disney Productions had on order and that, typically, was to be a model for the next generation of executive jets—a technological leader.

But the backyard train and the plane were in contrast with the essential Disney personality. The *Los Angeles Times*'s obituary editorial speculated that Disney's "real joy must have come from seeing the flash of delight sweep across a child's face and hearing his sudden laughter, at the first sight of Mickey Mouse, or Snow White or Pinocchio." Certainly the sight did not make him unhappy, but the *Times*' own biographical sketch, appearing in the same edition, carried a more nearly true statement from Disney himself on the source of his deepest satisfaction in his later years. A reporter once asked him, according to the piece, to name his most rewarding experience, and Disney's reply was blunt and brief: "The whole damn thing. The fact that I was able to build an organization and hold it . . ."

These are clearly not the words of some kindly old uncle who just loves to come to your child's birthday party and do his magic tricks and tell his jokes and find his kicks in the kiddies' laughter and applause and their parents' gratitude. Neither do they appear to bear much resemblance to anything we might expect from an artist looking back over his career. They represent, instead, the entrepreneurial spirit triumphant. They are the words of a man who has struggled hard to establish himself and his product; who has fought his way in from the fringes of his chosen industry to its center; who has gambled his own money and his own future on his own innovative inspirations and organizational intelligence and more than once has come close to losing his whole bundle. They are, most of all, the words of a man who at last is in possession of the most important piece of information a player in the only really important American game can obtain—the knowledge that he is a sure economic winner, that no matter what happens the chance of his being busted out of the game has been eliminated and that his accumulated winnings will surely survive him.

This knowledge was vouchsafed by Disney only late in life, but when it was, he was fond of working variations on the theme that money was merely a fertilizer, useful only to the degree that it could make new crops of ideas and enterprises grow. This is, of course, an image that anyone brought up in the spirit of the Protestant ethic would instantly appreciate and probably applaud; it is also an image that Freud, and more particularly his latter-day followers into the dark realms where the relationship between money and feces are explored, would quickly—probably too quickly—understand and explicate at dismal length. To a builder of Disney's character, though, money did in fact perform precisely the function he liked to describe, and its symbolic value was in good part just what it seemed most obviously to be—a measure of distances traveled, a way of keeping score.

Looking back, it is easy to see that Disney was neither a sold-out nor a sidetracked artist. He was a man who had obtained what he truly wanted: elevation—at least on the lower levels—to the ranks of the other great inventor-entrepreneurs of our industrial history. He was of the stuff of Ford and Edison, a man who could do everything a great entrepreneur is expected to do—dream and create and hold.

To see Disney as merely the proprietor of a mouse factory is to miss entirely his significance as a primary force in the expression and formation of the American mass consciousness. One must, at last, take him seriously, because whatever the literary content of his works, however immature his conscious vision of his own motives and achievements was, there was undeniably some almost mystic bond between himself and the moods and styles and attitudes of this people. He could not help but reflect and summarize these things in his almost every action. We have been taught to understand that the medium is the message, and it seems indubitable that there was a message in each of the media that Disney conquered, a message that transcended whatever he thought—or we thought—he was saying. When we seemed to demand an optimistic myth he gave us the unconquerable Mouse. When we seemed to demand the sense of continuity implicit in reminders of our past, he gave us fairy tales in a form we could easily accept. When we demanded neutral, objective factuality, he gave us the nature films. When, in a time of deep inner stress, we demanded another kind of unifying vision, he gave us a simplified and rosy-hued version of the small town and rural America that may have formed our institutions and our heritage but no longer forms us as individuals. When we demanded, at last, not formal statements but simply environments in which to lose ourselves, he gave us those in the amusement parks.

His statements were often vulgar. They were often tasteless, and they often exalted the merely technological over the sensitively humane. They were often crassly commercial, sickeningly sentimental, crudely comic. But the flaws in the Disney version of the American vision were hardly unique to him. They are flaws that have crept into it over decades, and they are the flaws almost universally shared by the nation's citizens.

Balanced against them must be the virtues he shared with his countrymen as well—his individualism, his pragmatism, his will to survive, his appreciation of the possibilities inherent in technological progress, despite the bad odor it often gives off today. Above all, there was the ability to build and build and build—never stopping, never looking back, never finishing—the institution that bears his name. There is creativity of a kind in this, and it is a creativity that is not necessarily of a lesser order than artistic creativity. "The American mechanizes as freely as an old Greek sculpted, as the Venetian painted," a 19th-century English observer of our life once said, and it is sheer attitudinizing not to see in our mechanized institutions one of the highest expressions of this peculiar genius of ours. These industrial institutions may ultimately be our undoing, but it is being blind to history not to see that they were our making as well. It is culturally blind not to see that Disney was a forceful and, in his special way, imaginative worker in this, our only great tradition. The only fitting honor to be paid him is to associate him firmly with it and not with some artistic tradition that was fundamentally alien to him and invoked standards inappropriate to the evaluation of of his accomplishments. The industrial and entrepreneurial tradition that both moved and sheltered him was neither more nor less flawed than he was.

And so there is a certain appropriateness about his last works. Film is, after all, a transitory thing, as all works of art are in comparison to that thing that every American knows to abide—the land. Or as we prefer to think of it, real estate. At heart, Disneyland is the very stuff of the American Dream—improved land, land with buildings and machinery on it, land that is increasing in value day by day, thanks to its shrewd development. With its success Disney realized the dream that had been denied his father and that had driven Disney as it drives so many of us. The day before he died, he lay in his hospital bed, staring at the ceiling, envisioning the squares of acoustical tile as a grid map of Disneyworld in Florida, saying things like, "This is where we'll put the monorail. And we'll run the highway right here." Truly, he had found The Magic Kingdom.

Typically, this was a secret he kept to himself. To be sure, he told anyone who bothered to inquire that he was not a producer of children's entertainment, that in fact he had never made a film or a television show or an exhibit at Disneyland that did not have, as its primary criterion of success, its ability to please him. And he often admitted that his great pleasure was the *business* he had built, not the products it created. But he—and most especially his organization—did nothing to discourage the misunderstanding of his work and his motives. And so much did we want to believe that he was a kind of Pied Piper whose principal delight was speaking, for altruistic and sentimental reasons, the allegedly universal language of childhood, so much did we *need* an essentially false picture of him, that the public clung to this myth almost as tightly as an eager Wall Street hugged to its gray flannel bosom the delightful reports on the recent economic performance of Walt Disney Productions. The commercial statistics were powerful enough to send the price of the stock to the highest levels in history *after* Disney died, even though the only foreboding its analysts expressed about it in the 1960s was based precisely on the fear of the founder's death and the inability of his executives to carry on in the great tradition. The myth of the Disney personality became similarly inflated after his passing. It was well expressed by the correspondent of *Paris Match* who, in an obituary cover story (Mickey was displayed in full color, crying), reached an unprecedented— and quite possibly fictive—mawkishness, with his description of the scene at the hospital on the day of Disney's death:

"At St. Joseph's Christmas party, the delighted children were applauding the trained dog act and singing 'Oh, Tannenbaum.'

"The hospital chaplain stepped out of the room where the successful life of Walt Disney had just come to an end.

"'Lying there, he looks like Gulliver with his dream menagerie gathered around him,' he whispered."

One likes to think that, however pleased Disney might have been by the sentiment, there was a secret recess of his mind where he kept a rather precise accounting of who he was and what he was. Ray Bradbury, the writer, once conceived the notion of having Disney run for mayor of Los Angeles on the not completely unreasonable ground that he was the only man with enough technological imagination to rationalize the sprawling mess the megalopolis had become. He journeyed out to the studio to put the idea to Disney, who was flattered but declined the opportunity. "Ray," he asked, "why should I run for mayor when I'm already king?"

And so he even managed to speak his own best epitaph, the one he always feared someone would speak for him. Like all his other works it seemed fanciful only at first glance. At heart, it was completely realistic.

3 Exploring Walt Disney World

Getting There

Walt Disney World has its own complete transportation system to get you wherever you want to go. Yet because the property is so extensive—more than 28,000 acres, 98 of them for the Magic Kingdom and another 260 for Epcot, and another 135 for Disney-MGM—the system can be a bit confusing, even for an experienced Disney visitor.

Best known is the elevated monorail that connects Disney World's biggest resorts and attractions. There are also extensive bus, motor launch, and ferry systems.

If you are staying at an on-site resort or a Walt Disney World Village hotel, or if you hold a three-park ticket, on-site transportation is free. If not, you can buy yourself unlimited transportation within Disney World for $2.50 a day.

By Car If you arrive at either the Magic Kingdom, Epcot Center, or Disney-MGM by car, there is a $4 parking charge. If you're staying at a Disney World hotel, show your guest ID for free parking.

Make sure to remember or write down exactly where you park; you'll have an awfully long wait before the sea of automobiles has departed and yours is the only one left. Trams make frequent trips between the parking areas and the park's turnstiles.

If your car won't start or it breaks down in Disney World, the **Car Care Center** (tel. 407/824–4813) near the Toll Plaza to the Magic Kingdom offers emergency road service. The center is open weekdays 7 AM–5:30 PM. The gas islands stay open 90 minutes after the Magic Kingdom closes. If you need to drop your car off to be serviced, there is free shuttle service around the park.

By Motor Launch These boats depart about every 20 minutes, and use color-coded flags to identify their route. They are for the use of resort guests only, with the exception of day guests with special activity tickets (i.e., to Discovery Island or River Country).

Blue—Connects the Contemporary Resort with the Fort Wilderness Resort Area and Discovery Island every 15 minutes between 9 AM and 10 PM.

Gold—Connects the Grand Floridian, Magic Kingdom, and Polynesian Resort at 15- to 25-minute intervals from 30 minutes before the Magic Kingdom opens until it closes, with pickup only from the Magic Kingdom until the park clears.

Green—Connects the Magic Kingdom, Fort Wilderness Resort Area, and Discovery Island (when it is open) every 20–25 minutes from half an hour before opening until closing time.

By Ferry A ferry service runs across Seven Seas Lagoon connecting the Transportation and Ticket Center (TTC) with the Magic Kingdom. The huge gleaming white crafts depart from each side of the lagoon about every 12 minutes when the Magic Kingdom is open. They can at times get you to the Magic Kingdom faster than the monorail. It is a comfortable ride, gliding over the lagoon's silky waters. Most people heading for the Magic Kingdom opt for the monorail and then take the ferry back at day's end for a chance to relax. If you want to avoid the worst of the lines for both monorail and ferry, take the opposite tack.

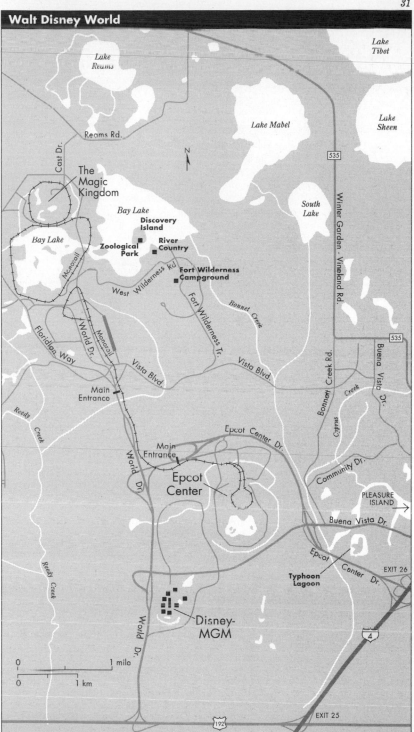

Lake Tibet

Lake Reams

Lake Mabel

Lake Sheen

Reams Rd.

Cast Dr.

The Magic Kingdom

Bay Lake

South Lake

Discovery Island

Bay Lake

Zoological Park

River Country

Fort Wilderness Campground

Monorail

West Wilderness Rd.

Fort Wilderness Tr.

Bonnet Creek

Winter Garden - Vineland Rd.

535

535

Floridian Way

World Dr.

Monorail

Vista Blvd.

Vista Blvd.

Bonnet Creek Rd.

Buena Vista Dr.

Cyprus Creek

Main Entrance

Reedy Creek

Main Entrance

Epcot Center Dr.

Community Dr.

Epcot Center

PLEASURE ISLAND →

Buena Vista Dr.

World Dr.

Reedy Creek

Epcot Center Dr.

EXIT 26

Typhoon Lagoon

Disney-MGM

4

0 _____ 1 mile

0 _____ 1 km

World Dr.

EXIT 25

192

EXIT 25

By Monorail This elevated train operates daily from 7:30 AM to 11 PM (or until one hour after the Magic Kingdom closes). The monorail does not go everywhere. It is a fun way to travel, and the air-conditioning is a godsend on a sweltering day; but be prepared for delays during busy periods because of mechanical problems or overcrowding.

The central connecting station for the monorail is called the **Transportation and Ticket Center** (TTC). One monorail line goes from the TTC to the Magic Kingdom and back in a loop around Seven Seas Lagoon. This is primarily for visitors who are not guests at the on-site resorts. Another line connects the TTC with the Contemporary Resort, the Magic Kingdom, the Grand Floridian, and the Polynesian. A third line goes directly from the TTC to Epcot. The TTC is where you can transfer between the Disney bus system and the monorail.

When you get to a monorail station ask an attendant if you can sit up in the conductor's cabin, called "the nose" by the crew. If there is room, the ride up front is much more exciting than sitting back in one of the regular cabins. It makes the kids feel important, and even adults will get a kick out of it.

By Tram Plans are for a tram to connect the four Epcot Center Resorts along the boardwalk with International Gateway, the new Epcot entrance behind France.

By Bus The bus system seems more complicated than it is. Each bus carries a small color-coded and/or letter-coded pennant on the front and sides. They come by at 15- to 25-minute intervals. Here's where they take you:

Green—Connects Disney Inn and Polynesian Village Resort with the TTC. This line operates from 7 AM to 2 AM. If there is an MK pennant on the bus, it connects Disney Inn with the Magic Kingdom and runs from 7 PM until two hours after the park closes.

Blue—Connects Fort Wilderness Resort Area with the TTC. These buses operate every 8 minutes from 7 AM to 2 AM.

Green-and-Gold—If the pennant has the letters EC on it, the bus connects Epcot, the Resort Villas, the Disney Village Marketplace, and Disney Village Clubhouse. If the bus has the letters MK on it, it travels only between the TTC and the villas. If the bus has ST/V on it, the bus connects Disney-MGM, Disney Village Marketplace, Pleasure Island, the Resort Villas, and Disney Village Clubhouse. These lines operate: EC 8 AM–2 AM; MK 7 AM–2 AM; and ST/V 8 AM–two hours after Disney-MGM closes, and 6 PM–2 AM to Pleasure Island.

Red-and-White—Connects Walt Disney World Village Hotel Plaza with the theme parks and Pleasure Island beginning at 8 AM and running until two hours after the respective parks close. Bus EC goes to Epcot, MK to the TTC for the Magic Kingdom, and ST goes to Disney-MGM. Bus V connects with Pleasure Island and Disney Village Marketplace and operates between 6 PM and 2 AM.

Red—Connects TTC, Disney Village Marketplace, Epcot, and Typhoon Lagoon between 8 AM and 2 AM. It includes Pleasure Island from 6 PM to 2 AM.

Gold—Connects the Grand Floridian, Polynesian Resort and Contemporary Resort with the TTC from 7 AM to 2 AM.

Orange-and-White Stripe—If the pennant has the letters MK on it, the bus connects Caribbean Beach Resort with the TTC from 7 AM until 2 AM. If the bus has the letters EC on it, it connects Epcot and Caribbean Beach Resort from 8 AM to two hours after Epcot closes. If the pennant is ST, the bus connects Caribbean Beach Resort with Disney-MGM from 8 AM to two hours after the park closes. If the letter is V, the bus connects the Caribbean Beach Resort with the Disney Marketplace and Typhoon Lagoon between 8 AM and 2:30 AM, and includes Pleasure Island from 6 PM to 2 AM.

Purple-and-Gold—These buses service the Epcot resorts: MK to TTC from 7 AM to 2 AM, and V to Disney Village Marketplace (8 AM–2 AM), Typhoon Lagoon (park hours), and Pleasure Island (6 PM–2 AM).

Gold-and-Black—The STE bus takes a Disney-MGM, Fort Wilderness, Contemporary Resort route; the STW bus stops at Disney-MGM, the Polynesian Village, the Grand Floridian, and Disney Inn. Both routes run from 8 AM until two hours after the park closes, and include Pleasure Island from 6 PM to 2 AM.

Blue-and-White—The EC connects Disney-MGM with Epcot, and the MK connects Disney-MGM with TTC. Both routes run from 8 AM to two hours after the parks close.

Brown—A Fort Wilderness Transportation Circle line. It connects Pioneer Hall, the Meadows Trading Post, Lodge/River Country parking lot, Creekside Meadows, and the Meadows complex with Loops 300, 500, 600, and 800–2800 from 7 AM to 2 AM.

Silver—Another Fort Wilderness Transportation Circle line. It connects Pioneer Hall, the Meadows Trading Post, Lodge/River Country parking lot, Creekside Meadows, and the Meadows complex with Loops 300, 500, 600, and 800–2800 from 7 AM to 2 AM.

Orange—The Caribbean Beach Resort internal transportation line, operates from 7 AM to 2 AM.

Orange (tram)—River Country to its parking lot, operating during River Country hours.

Admission

Visiting Walt Disney World is not cheap, especially if you have a child or two along. There are no discounted family tickets.

Sixteen different types of admission tickets are sold in one of two categories—adult, meaning everyone 10 and older, and children 3–9.

The word "ticket" is used by Disney World to mean only a single day's admission to the Magic Kingdom, Epcot, or the Disney-MGM Studios Theme Park. The price is $33 for adults and $26 for children. If you want to spend two or three days visiting the attractions, you have to buy a separate ticket each day. For more than three days, Disney World offers what it calls the All Three Parks Passport, which admits you to all three parks, along with unlimited use of the internal transportation system.

Here is a list of prices, tax not included. They are subject to change, so call for confirmation.

One-day ticket	$33 adults, $26 children
Four-day passport	$111 adults, $88 children
Five-day passport	$145 adults, $116 children
Six-day passport	$150 adults, $120 children
Annual Pass (new)	$180 adults, $155 children*
Annual Pass (renewal)	$160 adults, $135 children*
Annual Pass (charter renewal)	$140 adults, $115 children*
River Country, one day	$11.75 adults, $9.25 children; *$10.75/$8.25*
River Country, two days	$17.75 adults, $13.75 children; *$16.75/$12.75*
River Country annual pass	$50 adults and children
Combined River Country/Discovery Island, one day	$15 adults, $11 children; *$14/$10*
Discovery Island, one day	$8 adults, $4.50 children
Typhoon Lagoon, one day	$18.25 adults, $14.50 children; *$16.25/$13*
Typhoon Lagoon annual pass	$79.50 adults and children
Pleasure Island, one day	$9.95 adults and children
Pleasure Island, annual pass	$24.95 adults and children

*An additional $15 (adults) and $11 (children) entitles pass-holders to unlimited use of River Country and Discovery Island for the duration of their annual passes.

Italics indicates prices for visitors staying in a Disney World Resort or in a resort in the WDW Village Hotel Plaza.

Passports are available for four or five days. They can save you a great deal of money, and may be advisable even if you're staying in the area for only two days. Each time you use a passport the entry date is stamped on it; remaining days may be used any time in the future. If you buy a one-day ticket and later decide to extend your visit, you can get full credit for it toward the purchase of any passport. Exchanges can be made at City Hall in the Magic Kingdom, at Earth Station in Epcot, or at Guest Relations at Disney-MGM. Do this before leaving the park; once you've left, the ticket is worthless.

Tickets and passports to Disney World, Epcot Center, and Disney-MGM Studios Theme Park can be purchased at admission booths at the TTC, in all on-site resorts (if you're a registered guest), or at the Walt Disney World kiosk on the second floor of the main terminal at Orlando International Airport. If you want to buy them before arriving in Orlando, send a check or money order to Admissions, Walt Disney World, Box 10000, Lake Buena Vista, FL 32830. Remember, it usually takes four to six weeks for the order to be processed, so write well in advance.

If you want to leave the Magic Kingdom, Epcot, and Disney-MGM and return on the same day, be sure to have your hand stamped on the way out. You'll need your ticket *and* the handstamp to be readmitted.

Operating Hours

Operating hours for the Magic Kingdom, Epcot Center, and Disney-MGM Studios Theme Park vary widely throughout the year and change for school and legal holidays. In general, the longest days are during the prime summer months, when the Magic Kingdom is open to midnight, Epcot is open to 11 PM, and Disney-MGM is open to 9 PM.

At other times of the year, Epcot and Disney-MGM are open until 8 PM and the Magic Kingdom is open to 6 PM, with Main Street remaining open until 7.

It's important to remember that though the Magic Kingdom, Epcot, and Disney-MGM officially open at 9 AM, visitors may enter at 8:30, and sometimes at 8. The parking lots open at least an hour before the parks. Parking is $4 a day. Arriving before the official opening time, you can enjoy breakfast in the Magic Kingdom, make dinner reservations before the crowds arrive, and be among the first on line for the most popular attractions when they open at 9.

Ratings

Specific attractions in the Magic Kingdom, Epcot Center, and Disney-MGM Studios Theme Park have been rated according to general audience response to the quality of the ride or show, in comparison to other attractions within Disney World. Ratings do not indicate the size of the crowd that will be encountered at the particular attractions, but rather suggest how enjoyable visitors seem to regard the attractions. The following ratings were determined by sampling visitors' opinions as they departed the attractions:

Very popular (most enjoyable)
Popular
Moderately popular
Not very popular
Unpopular (least enjoyable)

At Epcot's World Showcase, the national pavilions are enjoyable for audiences of all ages; however, young children may consider this cultural fare less exciting than the fantasy oriented attractions at the Magic Kingdom, and they may find all the walking required an exhausting experience.

Magic Kingdom

When people think of Disney World, it is the Magic Kingdom that sparks their imaginations. This is the main event in Orlando, the center-ring attraction that draws millions of people to central Florida year after year. Mickey arm-in-arm with a joyful young guest beneath Cinderella's fairytale castle; jungle cruises and space mountains; cartoon characters dancing through a fantasyland as a high-pitched chorus sings refrains from "It's a Small World"—these are images that have burned their way into our national consciousness. The Magic Kingdom offers 45 major attractions in seven different "lands" spread across 98 acres. Many of the rides are geared for the young but most of them can be enjoyed by the young at heart. Even those who dread amusement parks can't help but be awed by the scope of Disney's vision.

Getting There

By car, take I–4 west to the clearly marked exit sign for the Magic Kingdom. This will put you on U.S. 192 W. It's a four-mile drive along Disney's main entrance road to the toll gate, and another mile to the huge parking area. Each of the 12 areas is named for a Disney cartoon character (Donald, Pluto, etc.) and every parking space has its own number. Tractor-drawn trams pass frequently through the parking areas and whisk you to the monorail and ferry, which will take you to the gates of the Kingdom.

If you are staying at one of the Disney hotels, *see* Getting There, at the beginning of this chapter, for transportation connecting hotels to the Magic Kingdom.

It's an arduous journey just getting to the gates of the Magic Kingdom (during summer or other busy seasons, be prepared for serious bumper-to-bumper traffic both on I–4 nearing the U.S. 192 exit and on 192 itself), but this is the way Walt Disney wanted it. When Disneyland opened in California, the lush orange groves that surrounded the park soon turned into an ugly mass of commercial development. Disney did not want this to happen at the Orlando site, so he surrounded his Magic Kingdom with a broad buffer zone of forests and fields. Disney also wanted to create in visitors the effect of leaving their work-a-day lives behind.

Orientation

Numbers in the margin correspond with points of interest on the Magic Kingdom map.

The first plaza you enter is Town Square. City Hall and Sun Bank are on your left; Hospitality House, Tony's Town Square Cafe, and the Walt Disney Story—Disney memorabilia and a movie depicting Walt's life—are on your right; behind you is the Walt Disney World Railroad station with lockers and strollers. Stretching before you is Main Street—a boulevard filled with Victorian-style stores and dining spots. Walk two blocks along Main Street, and you will enter Central Plaza with Cinderella Castle rising up directly in front of you. This is the hub of the Kingdom; all of the "lands" radiate out from it, like wedges of a pie. Town Square is the starting point of the daily parade (usually 3–3:20 PM) of cartoon characters.

On your immediate left as you stand in the center of Central Plaza is a bridge leading to Adventureland, where you will find the Jungle Cruise, Pirates of the Caribbean, and a few other attractions. To your left, and a bit ahead, is a bridge leading to Frontierland and Liberty Square. These two smaller lands offer Big Thunder Mountain Railroad, Haunted Mansion, boat rides, and other shows. Adventureland, Frontierland, and Liberty Square are the lands with the greatest appeal for adults.

❶ Cinderella Castle. Directly in front of you, as you stand in Central Plaza, is a passageway through the castle to Fantasyland. All the rides here are primarily for children, with the exception of 20,000 Leagues Under the Sea, which is recommended for visitors of all ages.

To the right of the Cinderella Castle is a path that takes you to the border between Fantasyland and Tomorrowland and straight through to Mickey's Starland. Cross the bridge on your immediate right and you're in Tomorrowland, with little of interest to most visitors except for the dizzying Space Mountain ride.

Paths take you from one neighboring land to the next; however, if you want to get to a land that is "two or more wedges of the pie away," it may be faster to go back through Central Plaza. You can also take advantage of the Swiss-made Skyway gondola that connects the Liberty Square side of Fantasyland to Tomorrowland. The Skyway offers a bird's-eye view of these two lands, but it is not exactly rapid transportation.

It's not as long a walk from one land to the next as you might think, but don't think you can do the whole Kingdom in a day. Even if the crowds are small, see what interests you most and plan to return later. Remember, the early morning and late evening are the times when you can see and do the most.

Town Square

❷ City Hall. First stop in Town Square should be City Hall, which will be on your left, next to Sun Bank. City Hall has an information desk where you can pick up the *Magic Kingdom Guide Book* and a schedule of daily events (you should save time by getting a copy in advance at a Disney hotel or writing for one before you leave home). City Hall has a lost-and-found both for property and for people. Should anyone in your party get lost or separated, this is where to go. Nearby, beneath the Railroad, are coin deposit lockers where bags, stuffed animals, and so on can be stored.

❸ WDW Railroad. A great way to get an overview of the Kingdom is to hop aboard the Railroad and take a 14-minute, 1.5-mile ride around the entire perimeter of the park. You can board at the Victorian-style station that you pass beneath to enter Town Square. Until recently, the only other station was in Frontierland. A new station has been built to provide access to Mickey's Birthdayland on the border between Tomorrowland and Fantasyland.

The train is pulled by a steam engine that was built in Philadelphia in 1916. It was brought to Disney World from the Yucatán

Cinderella Castle, **1**
City Hall, **2**
WDW Railroad, **3**
Jungle Cruise, **4**
Pirates of the
Caribbean, **5**
Big Thunder Mountain
Railroad, **6**
Country Bear, **7**
Tom Sawyer Island, **8**
Fort Sam Clemens, **9**
Haunted Mansion, **10**
Hall of Presidents, **11**
20,000 Leagues, **12**
It's a Small World, **13**
Space Mountain, **14**
American
Journeys, **15**
Grand Prix, **16**
Mickey's House, **17**
Mickey's Hollywood
Theatre, **18**
Grandma Duck's
Farm, **19**

The Magic Kingdom

FRONTIERLAND

Railroad
Station

ADVENTURELAND

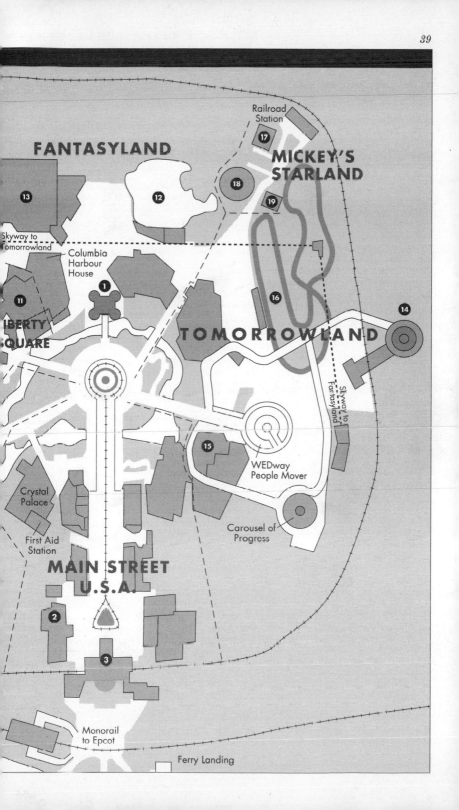

FANTASYLAND

Railroad
Station

17

MICKEY'S
STARLAND

18

12

13

19

Skyway to
Tomorrowland

Columbia
Harbour
House

1

11

16

LIBERTY
SQUARE

TOMORROWLAND

14

Skyway to
Fantasyland

15

WEDway
People Mover

Crystal
Palace

First Aid
Station

Carousel of
Progress

MAIN STREET
U.S.A.

2

3

Monorail
to Epcot

Ferry Landing

Peninsula of Mexico, where early in the century it was used to transport sugarcane.

Main Street

The atmosphere is Hollywood Victorian in this Disney version of small-town America. Behind the facades are clothing and gift shops circa 1990. At least four points of interest are more than skin-deep.

The Walt Disney Story. On the right (east) side of Town Square, opposite City Hall, is a yellow Victorian house where a film and some Disney memorabilia offer insights into Disney's life and the empire he created.

Main Street Vehicles. A little red fire engine, a horseless carriage, a jitney, an omnibus, even a horse-drawn trolley are among the vehicles you can ride free along the street.

Main Street Cinema. On your right as you leave Town Square and walk toward Cinderella Castle is a silent-movie house that shows several films simultaneously on five screens—everything from Disney's earliest Mickey Mouse cartoons to slapstick, Keystone Kops-type flicks. This is entertaining for adults, a cool retreat from the heat, and seldom too crowded.

Penny Arcade. Midway down Main Street, on the left, is a large game room with everything from moving-picture boxes and player pianos to the newest high-tech electronic video games. Quarters will be consumed here as fast as you can put them into your children's hands. Adults can spend a small fortune, too, on the old-fashioned Kiss-O-Meters.

Adventureland

These soft adventures to far-off lands are among the most crowded in the Kingdom. Visit first thing in the morning or as late in the afternoon as possible, or, better yet, in the evening.

Swiss Family Robinson Treehouse. *Popular; all ages.* The first attraction you will see is an outdoor, walk-through exhibit showing how the Swiss Family Robinson might have lived on their tropical island. Visitors walk up stairs and ramps into a realistic-looking tree made of cement and metal. It can take five minutes or as long as 25 minutes to pass through in single file. If there is a line, you may want to leave the family on their island, move on to the Jungle Cruise, and come back, say, after dinner.

❹ Jungle Cruise. *Very popular; all ages.* Canopied explorer launches take visitors on a journey along the Nile, through an Amazon rain forest, across an African jungle, and so on. Along the way you pass through a world of angry hippopotami, roaring lions, hungry cannibals, and bathing elephants that spray your boat. Good thing you have a tour guide to protect you through these treacherous waters and humor you with stories of less fortunate passengers who never made it through the journey. Kids eat it up, and everyone is amused. The ride itself takes only 10 minutes, but the line can take as long as an hour. Go as soon as the park opens, during the parade time (3–3:20 PM), or after 5 PM. Avoid 10 AM to noon.

❺ Pirates of the Caribbean. *Very popular; all ages.* Journey through a world of pirate strongholds and treasure-filled dungeons as G-rated seafarers swig their booze, sing chanteys, and revel in their booty and their women. The special effects, complete with Audio-Animatronics pirates and animals, are first class. Lines fluctuate throughout the day, but move fairly quickly. Best time is 2–3:30 PM and after 5 PM. Avoid 10 AM to noon.

Tropical Serenade—Enchanted Tikki Birds. *Not very popular, but still crowded; for children.* These were the first Audio-Animatronics creations, and it shows. The ceiling is covered with hundreds of exotic birds that jest and sing, but it is difficult to tell which bird is talking at any given time and even children find the show a bit confusing and not one of the park's top attractions. The tropical backdrop is worth a look—but you have to see the show to do so.

Frontierland

"Frontier Fun" is the theme of this gold-rush town of the Southwest.

6 Big Thunder Mountain Railroad. *Very popular;* children must be at least 4'2". As rollercoasters go, the ride is tame. But it's fun and exciting, nonetheless, to pitch and swerve around hills and into valleys, through a coal mine, a gold digger's settlement, and a ghost town. It's a fast, fun ride that is sure to get your heart pounding. It's also one of only two fast rides in the park (the other is Space Mountain). Try to go in the evening when the mountain is all lit up and lines are relatively short. Don't confuse this ride with the Walt Disney World Railroad that has a station in Frontierland.

7 Country Bear Jamboree. *Moderately popular; all ages.* This is an unabashedly corny stage show in which furry Audio-Animatronics bears joke, sing, and play down-home, country music and 1950s rock 'n' roll. It is a show for children or for anyone who loves puns.

Diamond Horseshoe Jamboree. *Popular; all ages.* An Old-Western saloon is the setting for this live stage show featuring all sorts of singing, dancing, and innocently rowdy entertainment. Sandwiches and light refreshments may be purchased before curtain time. You must make reservations early in the morning at the Hospitality House on Main Street because there are only five shows a day. Reservations are handed out on a first-come, first-served basis, with the strongest demand usually for the 12:15 show. Other shows are at 10:45 AM and 1:45, 3:30 and 4:45 PM. dinner

8 Tom Sawyer Island. *Not very popular; all ages.* A raft takes you across the Rivers of America to an island where walking paths **9** lead to a cave, a couple of bouncy bridges, and **Fort Sam Clemens.** There is not much to see, but a sojourn here is a pleasant respite from the crowded mainland.

Liberty Square

This small land adjoins and blends into Frontierland. Its theme is Colonial History, and it consists of Early American-style shops and eating places. It has a few decent but tame attractions. Don't miss the chocolate chip cookies at the Snackspot next to Heritage House.

⑩ **Haunted Mansion.** *Very popular; all ages.* Ghosts and goblins haunt you at every turn through this eerie world of attics, dungeons, and graveyards. The special effects can seem very realistic and the buggies you ride in swivel from side to side. This attraction is not exactly frightening, but young children might disagree. It is one of the most imaginative attractions in the park. The best time to go is in the early morning or evening. Avoid noon–4 PM.

Liberty Square Riverboats. *Moderately popular; all ages.* This is a low-key attraction that takes you on an authentic-looking paddlewheel steamboat for a half-mile cruise through the "Rivers of America," passing along the way a series of reenacted scenes from the Wild West. It's not great entertainment, but it can be a comfortable escape from the crowds and the sun.

⑪ **Hall of Presidents.** *Moderately popular; adults or mature children.* When it first opened, this theatrical portrait of Presidents past and present caused quite a sensation because it was here that the first refinements of the Audio-Animatronics system could be seen in action. Although the show may now seem a bit slow and unexciting, it is interesting to hear the Disney view of American history and watch the seemingly immobile Presidents suddenly stand. Young children may find it boring, and if you have seen American Adventure at Epcot, you may, too. However, you may enjoy brushing up on a few major episodes in our nation's history, and the figures are strikingly realistic. Arrive several minutes before the show begins so you can take a look at the many historical artifacts on display in the rotunda, such as Revolutionary-era flags, muskets, and portraits.

Fantasyland

This is a land in which storybook dreams come true, and young children are very much in their element. The rides are all quite mild. There are a few traditional amusement-park rides with Disney themes, such as the **Mad Tea Party,** where teacups spin around a big tea pot. Other favorites are **Dumbo the Flying Elephant** and a spectacular merry-go-round. There are several other indoor rides that spook and enchant children as they pass through a cartoon world filled with many familiar fairytale characters. Fantasyland is not exclusively for children, though; several attractions will interest adults as well.

⑫ **20,000 Leagues Under the Sea.** *Very popular; all ages.* Inspired by the Jules Verne novel, this is one of the most popular attractions in the park, and one of the most elaborate. The notorious Captain Nemo takes you in his tightly packed Nautilus submarine to explore a beautiful and dangerous undersea world full of curious aquatic creatures. As the submarine circles the lagoon and penetrates a treacherous cavern, passengers gaze out through submerged portholes at lifelike vegetation, fish, tortoises, divers, and even a giant killer squid. Looking out through the portholes, you really do feel as though you are penetrating the ocean depths. There isn't much action in these waters, but it is quite a spectacle, and quite a vessel. Lines move very slowly, so go the first thing in the morning or late in the evening.

Magic Journeys. *Popular; all ages.* Put on a pair of 3-D glasses and have fun with the illusion of being bombarded by images that seem to fly at you from off the movie screen. After standing in a small, cramped room to watch a brief Disney 3-D cartoon from the 1930s, visitors move into another theater where they sit to watch the main event—a rather ingenuous film made for Epcot Center's Imagination Pavilion about some children's fantasy of joining a circus. The premise is fatuous, but sweet, and children enjoy it.

Mr. Toad's Wild Ride, Snow White's Adventures, Peter Pan's Flight. *Popular; for younger children.* These are all very similar types of indoor rides that take children on fairytale adventures. Both Mr. Toad and Snow White have many startling noises and scary images that may frighten very young children. Peter Pan's Flight is a great ride in the sky for children of all ages. The flight to Never-Never Land over moonlit London is spectacular, and so are many of the other special effects created with black light, fluorescent paint, and a lot of imagination.

⑬ It's a Small World. *Very popular; young children.* In this famous attraction originally created for New York's 1964–65 World's Fair, gaily dancing and singing puppets garbed in colorful native dress from many nations convey the timeless hope for peace and harmony in the world. The background music is sing-song but unforgettable, and the idea is positively saccharine. But kids love it nonetheless.

Tomorrowland

"Fun in the Future" is the motto of this section. Save it for the future if your time is limited; except for Space Mountain, all the rides are pretty unspectacular. The major problem is that what in 1970 was a look into the future now often seems rather dated. Another problem is that most of the attractions are sponsored by large corporations, and the audience is bombarded by commercial advertising at every turn. Visitors who want this sort of entertainment can get it at home, sitting on their living-room couches; or they can see better versions of it over at Epcot.

Despite its limitations, however, Tomorrowland has some redeeming traits. A few of the rides are fun for young children, and Space Mountain is an exciting ride for anybody who has the stomach for it. Also, the lines in this land are among the shortest.

⑭ Space Mountain. *Very popular; children must be at least 3; children under 7 must be accompanied by an adult.* This space-age, cone-shaped building is a landmark in the Kingdom. The roller coaster may never get to speeds over 20 miles per hour, but the experience in the dark, with everyone screaming and "stars" and "meteors" all around, is thrilling, even for hardcore roller coaster fans. Don't take any loose objects on the ride with you, because your hands will be too busy holding on and objects can easily fall out of cars as they dip and turn. You may even want to hold on to your children's wallets while they ride. To see the interior without taking the ride, hop aboard the People Mover.

⑮ American Journeys, Carousel of Progress, Mission to Mars. *Unpopular; all ages.* Each attraction lasts some 20 minutes and for some of you it will be 20 minutes too long. *Mission to Mars* is a theatrical, two-part, standing-and-sitting journey to Mars, taking you from the mission control room to your blast-off chamber where you watch some rather tired 7th-grade vintage film footage of outer space. *Carousel of Progress* is a theater that revolves around a series of stages with Audio-Animatronics characters that depict the evolution of technology in the American home through the 20th century. *American Journeys*, a film in CircleVision with nine movie screens, takes a patriotic look at the landscape of America. It is scheduled to be replaced this year by a new movie on the culture of Western civilization.

Dreamflight. *Popular; all ages*. This attraction takes you on a ride through the history of aviation.

Starjets. *Moderately popular; for children*. These are small planes that circle around a rocket tower, rising and dipping as they go. Pleasant, but not worth waiting in a long line to experience.

16 Grand Prix Raceway. *Popular; children must be at least seven to go alone*. Mini race cars sputter along a winding tract at breathtaking speeds of up to seven miles per hour. The cars are guided along rails but have their own steering and brakes. Children who do not meet age and height requirements must be accompanied by adults.

Mickey's Starland

Built to celebrate Mickey Mouse's 60th birthday in 1988, the newest of the Magic Kingdom's lands is a big hit with children. Guests catch the railroad at Main Street or Frontierland and take it to Duckburg, where they can view some of Mickey's famous cartoons and films, visit Mickey's house, meet Mickey for some photos, and join in Mickey's surprise birthday party, which has even the adults laughing when they leave. For parents who want to rest their feet, there is a playground, a petting zoo, and a maze for the children.

17 Mickey's House. *Popular; for younger children*. Stroll through the house and enjoy the memorabilia. When you walk out the back door, you are in the birthday party tent, where you catch some old film clips, help Minnie in the kitchen, and enjoy the surprise party thrown for Mickey by his buddies. The children will love it.

18 Mickey's Hollywood Theatre. *Very popular; for younger children*. Here is a chance to have your children pose with Mickey in an orderly one-on-one opportunity, rather than trying to fight the crowds throughout the park when Mickey is spotted strolling around.

19 Grandma Duck's Farm. *Moderately popular; for children*. You will never again see a farmyard so clean, but there are real barnyard babies to pet.

Time Out Visitors who care about real food will discover that gourmet dining is as much a fantasy as everything else in the Magic Kingdom. Fast food is king, and even the few sit-down, full-service restaurants are more like themed coffee shops than serious places to dine. What you will find are plenty of snack stands with hamburgers, hot dogs, pizza, pastries, cookies, and burritos. Visitors may want to create their own picnic lunches from a deli outside the Kingdom, store it in one of the lockers beneath the Railroad Station in Town Square, and eat it on a park bench or at a table in a fast-food joint. If you want to sit down to a meal, there are a few places to go. Lunch entrees range from $5 to $10, and dinner entrees range from $15 to $20. If you have just a day to spend and are visiting during a busy season, grab a bite on the run around 11–11:30. If you have two days for the Magic Kingdom, consider leaving the park at noon and going to one of the hotels for a leisurely, civilized lunch.

Restaurants providing full service:

Fantasyland—King Stefan's Banquet Hall. Prime ribs, pot pies, and salads are served in a medieval Denny's-style dining hall upstairs in Cinderella Castle. If you really want to eat here, make reservations at the restaurant as soon as you arrive at the Kingdom.

Liberty Square—Liberty Tree Tavern. Located in the heart of Liberty Square, this colonial New England–themed restaurant serves chowder, sandwiches, and salads for lunch, and more hearty American fare for dinner. Make reservations here when you arrive at the Kingdom.

Main Street—Tony's Town Square Cafe. The decor is right out of *Lady and the Tramp*. The café serves full breakfasts, including Mickey Mouse waffles, and lunches and dinners of Italian dishes, burgers, chicken, fish, and steak.

Plaza Restaurant. For lunch, dinner, or just a treat from the soda fountain, try this bright, art nouveau–theme restaurant at the end of Main Street.

Although not table-service restaurants, other notable nooks for nourishment include:

Frontierland—Aunt Polly's Landing. There are sandwiches to munch and shade to enjoy on a covered porch while your youngsters romp on nearby Tom Sawyer Island.

Main Street—The Crystal Palace. A wide assortment of cafeteria food, including chicken, fish, prime rib, and salads, is served in a Victorian setting with patio seating.

Tomorrowland—Launching Pad. If you have had your fill of junk food, here is a place to get health foods.

Tomorrowland Terrace. You can always find a place to sit down and eat in this large snack stop. It serves salads, sandwiches, and soups.

Epcot Center

The attractions at Epcot are designed more for thoughtful adults and curious children than for the fantasy- or thrill-seeking crowd.

The word Epcot stands for Experimental Prototype Community of Tomorrow—a misleadingly formal title for a park filled with many enjoyable and accessible rides and displays that do more to explain our past and present than to predict the future.

The idea for Epcot was conceived by Walt Disney himself more than 30 years ago. His thought was to create a place that, as he said, "will take its cue from the new ideas and technologies that are now emerging from the creative centers of American industry." Disney wanted to be sure that his center kept pace with corporate research and development. It will be, he said, "a community of tomorrow that will never be completed, but will always be introducing and testing and demonstrating new materials and systems." Disney's vision was noble, but what was meant to be a city of tomorrow became little more than a showcase of technology. Still, Future World has enough awe-inspiring attractions to engage even the most incurious of adults and children.

Getting There

Take I–4 west from Orlando to the sign marked Epcot Center. If you're coming from the Contemporary, Grand Floridian, or Polynesian Village resorts, hop aboard the monorail to the TTC station and follow signs for Epcot. If you're coming from the Magic Kingdom, take the monorail to the TTC and catch the train to Epcot. The 2.5-mile ride from the TTC is enjoyable because the train loops through Future World, Epcot's northern half, providing a dynamic overview of what you'll soon be seeing and doing. Everybody ooh's and aah's at his first aerial sight of the spectacular grounds.

By Bus If you are staying on Disney property, *see* Getting There, at the beginning of this chapter.

Orientation

Numbers in the margin correspond with points of interest on the Epcot Center map.

Epcot Center is divided almost equally into two distinct areas separated by the 40-acre World Showcase Lagoon. The northern half, which is where the admission gates are, is filled with the Future World pavilions, sponsored by major American corporations. The southern half is World Showcase.

If you want to minimize time spent waiting on lines, do the opposite of what most people do. In the morning visitors head for what's closest, which is Future World, so you should make a beeline for World Showcase. In the afternoon, come back and explore Future World while the crowds have shifted over to World Showcase. Evening hours, of course, are the best times for visiting either section of Epcot.

Future World

Future World is made up of two concentric circles of modern buildings. The inner circle consists of two crescent-shape buildings. As you enter, CommuniCore East will be on your left and CommuniCore West will be on your right. The outer circle has seven separate buildings, each featuring a technological theme sponsored by an American corporation.

Be methodical as you visit the attractions in Future World. If you skip around too much you may become disoriented and miss some of the best attractions.

❶ Earth Station—Epcot Information Center. Here, beneath the silvery geosphere, is a sensible place to begin your visit to Epcot. Lunch and dinner reservations can be secured, and questions answered. You can also get maps and entertainment schedules, and arrange for guided tours. Numerous two-way video TV screens, called Worldkey Information Satellites, allow you to see and ask questions of Epcot hosts and hostesses. Merely touch a computer screen and you can summon all sorts of information in several languages. In the Entrance Plaza, before you get to Earth Station, you will find a Sun Bank office, a camera shop, a stroller and wheelchair rental office, and a lost-and-found. Should anyone in your party get lost or separated, he or she should make his or her way to the Information Desk at Earth Station.

❷ Spaceship Earth. *Very popular; all ages.* This 17-story silver geosphere—some refer to it as a silver golf ball—is the first thing one sees on approaching Epcot. Visible from upper floors of hotels as far as 15 miles away, it is the very symbol of Future World.

Don't let the names confuse you: Earth Station is the Information Center located at the exit to the ride; Spaceship Earth is the ride inside the geosphere itself.

Sponsored by AT&T, Spaceship Earth traces the history of communication. It is a journey through time, beginning with prehistoric wall paintings and continuing through the space age. The familiar voice that narrates your tour belongs to Walter Cronkite. This is one of the most crowded attractions, so try to arrive as soon as Epcot opens or late in the evening.

❸ Universe of Energy. *Very popular; all ages.* Sponsored by Exxon, this attraction educates audiences in the origins and different forms of energy. It is called a Traveling Theater because entire rooms shift about as visitors travel through a world of Audio-Animatronics dinosaurs and enter a screening room to learn how energy is created and used.

❹ Wonders of Life. *Very popular; all ages.* Housed under a 60-foot gold dome, this newest of Disney's Future World exhibits, sponsored by MetLife, combines a thrill ride, a theater, and hands-on activities. The longest lines are for a 15-minute movie, *The Making of Me*, in a 100-seat theater. The movie explores, with spectacular film footage, reproduction, pregnancy, and birth. Because of the sensitive nature of the film, you might want to consider if you want to take your very young children in to see it. Everybody leaves the pavilion talking about Body Wars, a thrilling simulated ride through the immune system of the human body. You sit in a 40-passenger

Earth Station, **1**
Spaceship Earth, **2**
Universe of Energy, **3**
Wonders of Life, **4**
Horizons, **5**
World of Motion, **6**
Journey into
Imagination, **7**
The Land, **8**
The Living Seas, **9**
Communicore West, **10**
Communicore East, **11**
Mexico, **12**
Norway, **13**
China, **14**
Germany, **15**
Italy, **16**
American
Adventure, **17**
Japan, **18**
Morocco, **19**
France, **20**
United Kingdom, **21**
Canada, **22**

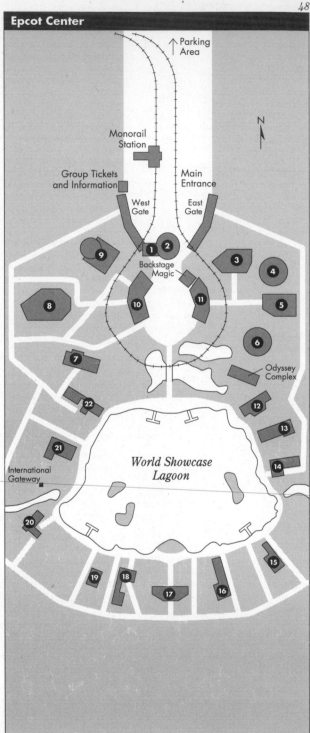

Epcot Center

flight simulator, and the ride is pretty rough. The theater production, *Cranium Command*, is another popular attraction in which viewers sit in the head of a 12-year-old as he goes through a day of his life. It's a sneaky stress-management lesson. The other features include *Goofy About Health*, a multiscreen video presentation about good health habits, starring Goofy; AnaComical Players, an improvisational theater troupe that involves guests in humorous skits; Coach's Corner, where your baseball, golf, or tennis swing is analyzed; Frontiers of Medicine, exhibits of the latest developments in medicine and health sciences; Met Lifestyle Revue, an opportunity for you to get a computer-generated analysis of your health habits; Sensory Funhouse, hands-on learning experiences using the five senses; and Wondercycles, exercise bikes set up with a video tour. Even the food, such as whole-grain waffles with fresh fruit toppings, is healthful in here.

⑤ Horizons. *Popular; all ages.* Four-passenger vehicles give visitors a look at the inventions of yesterday, and then convey them into an OmniSphere where on a pair of hemispherical screens they are treated to a look into the world of tomorrow, with scenes of a space-shuttle launch, life in a space colony, trains that work by magnetic levitation, and so on. General Electric is the sponsor.

⑥ World of Motion. *Moderately popular; all ages.* Sponsored by General Motors, the attraction itself is a rather fanciful, sketchy look at the history of transportation through the ages. The most informative part, Transcenter—you can see it without taking the ride—is a series of displays of vehicles of the future designed by General Motors.

⑦ Journey into Imagination. *Popular; for children.* Here is where you are introduced to Figment, the popular purple creature. Kids in particular are captivated by the elaborate and colorful trio of attractions that explore the creative process—a ride, a film, and a playground of electric sights and sounds called *Image Works*, where children and adults can exercise their imaginations.

Also in this building is the Captain EO 3-D movie starring pop singer Michael Jackson. There isn't much of a plot to this 17-minute *Star Wars*-type film, but the visual effects are wild. So realistic are the 3-D effects that almost everyone in the audience tries to reach out and touch the images that seem to fly off the screen.

The movie and ride are worth the wait in line, but try to go in the late afternoon when there are fewer people to contend with. Be sure not to miss the "dancing waters" fountains in front of the exit to Captain EO. They are especially entertaining after dark.

⑧ The Land. Sponsored by Kraft, this building hosts the most educational attractions in Future World for both young and older audiences.

Listen to the Land. Popular; for adults and mature children. The main event in the building is a boat ride through an experimental greenhouse that demonstrates how plants may be grown in the future, not only on Earth but in outer space. This is the most educationally valuable ride in all of Disney World. Some kids may find it dull, but adults are usually impressed. If the experience inspires you to learn more about these processes, you can arrange to join one of the walking tours, guided by professional researchers, that depart a dozen or so times a day. Reservations should be made in the morning on the lower floor, in the corner opposite the boat ride entrance, behind Broccoli and Company (a shop).

Harvest Theater. Moderately popular; all ages. A beautiful 19-minute nature film called "Symbiosis" shows how people interact with their environment in different ways.

Kitchen Kabaret. Popular; for children. This is a very cute, sunny, Audio-Animatronics show for children about nutrition and the food groups, hosted by Bonnie Appetit and featuring dancing fruits and vegetables, and singing dairy products and meats. Adults with only one day in Epcot may want to skip it. Kids will love it, though.

❾ The Living Seas. *Popular; all ages.* Venture into the last frontier on Earth as you peer into this massive 5.7-million-gallon aquarium filled with some 8,000 sea creatures, including dolphins and sea lions and the divers who are training them. This serious research facility also features many educational exhibits and interactive displays that inquisitive visitors could spend a good half day exploring.

❿ ⓫ CommuniCore East and West. These two buildings house exhibits by Epcot's various sponsor companies. There are enough educational computer games to keep an inquisitive mind busy for days, learning how computers work, how energy is generated, how communications systems operate, and much, much more.

Epcot Outreach. This is a resource center in CommuniCore West that provides information and reference material on any subject showcased at Epcot.

World Showcase

The Showcase presents an ideal image—a Disney version—of life in 11 countries. Native food, entertainment, and wares are on display in each of the pavilions. Most of the nations have done an imaginative and painstaking job of re-creating scale models of their best-known monuments, such as the Eiffel Tower in France, a Mayan temple in Mexico, and a majestic pagoda in Japan. During the day these structures are impressive enough, but at night, when the darkness inhibits one's ability to judge size, one gets the sense that he is seeing the real thing. It's a wonderful illusion, indeed.

Unlike Future World and the Magic Kingdom, the Showcase doesn't offer amusement-park-type rides (except in Mexico and Norway). Instead, it features breathtaking films, ethnic art, cultural entertainment, Audio-Animatronics presentations, and dozens of shops and restaurants featuring national specialities.

You will find that some of the most enjoyable diversions in World Showcase are not inside the national pavilions but in their courtyards and on their streets under the open skies. At varying times of the day, each pavilion offers some sort of live street show, featuring comedy, song, dance, or mime routines, or demonstrations of folk arts and crafts. All performers, craftspeople, and other workers in the pavilions are natives of, or have ancestors from, one of the 11 countries; all are in the U.S. on a cultural exchange program and all speak English and often other languages as well. Don't be shy about exercising or trying to improve your language skills in their native tongues. Teenagers studying French, say, get a charge out of practicing their language skills in France or Morocco.

The only unfortunate note in this cultural smorgasbord is that, with so many shops and restaurants, there seems to be more of an emphasis on commercialism than on education or entertainment. There are many tasteful things to buy, but know in advance that a taste of a nation may mean a bite out of your bank account.

There are three ways of navigating World Showcase: (1) walk from pavilion to pavilion, (2) hop aboard the slow-moving double-decker buses that depart every five to eight minutes and stop in front of every other "nation," or (3) cruise across the lagoon in one of the air-conditioned 65-foot water taxis that depart every 12 minutes. When you first reach the shore of the lagoon closest to Future World, you'll see docks on both your right and your left. The water taxi leaving from the dock on your left travels to the Germany pavilion; the one on the right goes to Morocco. From either stop, you can walk to adjoining pavilions or hop a bus. It's more than a mile around the lagoon, so consider renting strollers for young children, either on the left side of Epcot's Entrance Plaza or at the International Gateway, next to France.

The Pavilions The focal point of World Showcase, on the opposite side of the lagoon from the Epcot entrance area, is the host pavilion, the **American Adventure,** sponsored by American Express and Coca-Cola—two symbolic giants of America, both at home and abroad. The pavilions of the other countries fan out from the right and left of American Adventure, encircling the lagoon.

Going clockwise from the left as you enter World Showcase are the pavilions of Mexico, Norway, People's Republic of China, Germany, Italy, American Adventure, Japan, Morocco, France, United Kingdom, and Canada. Apart from the shops and restaurants, here are some of the main attractions at each pavilion.

⑫ Mexico. *Moderately popular.* The "River of Time" boat ride inside the pavilion may remind some of "It's a Small World" in the Magic Kingdom, with the major tourist attractions of Mexico as its theme. Windows and doorways are filled with colorful video images, rooms are full of dancing, costumed puppets and landscapes that roar, storm, and light up as you journey from the jungles of the Yucatán to the skyline of Mexico City.

The building in which this pavilion is housed is in the form of an ancient Mayan temple similar to those found in the Yucatán. Upon entering the pavilion, visitors pass through a gallery of Spanish colonial art featuring portraits of conquistadores and religious 16th-century artifacts. Inside there is a *mercado* with colorful textiles, straw items, pottery, other Mexican handicrafts, and wandering mariachi bands. In front of the pavilion, outside, is **Cantina de San Angel**—a fast-food joint and bar that's good for burritos, margaritas, and—at night—a great view of the laser show, IllumiNations.

⑬ **Norway.** *Very popular.* Visitors take a ride in small Viking vessels through the landscape and history of this Scandinavian country. You can tour a 10th-century Viking Village, sail through a fjord, and experience a storm and the Midnight Sun.

The main spectacle of this pavilion is a re-creation of a 14th-century coastal fortress in Oslo called Akershus. Also special is a film that takes visitors on a tour of the country's architectural and natural highlights.

⑭ **China.** *Very popular.* The film "Wonders of China" should not be missed. It is a CircleVision presentation on the landscape of the country, taking viewers on a fantastic journey from Inner Mongolia to the Tibetan mountains, along the Great Wall, into Beijing, and through some of the most glorious landscapes on Earth.

The Chinese pavilion also features the "House of Whispering Willows," an exhibit of ancient Chinese art that is worth strolling through, and a large shopping gallery, Bountiful Harvest, that is practically a museum in its own right. Browse among ivory goods, jade jewelry and sculpture, hand-painted fans, opulent carpets, and inlaid furniture ranging in price from a few cents to thousands of dollars.

⑮ **Germany.** *Moderately popular.* The main event in this replica of a small Bavarian village is the oompah band show in the Biergarten restaurant, with singers, dancers, and musicians. The shops are also worth a quick look. There are four shows daily. You'll also find plenty of German wines, sweets, glassware, porcelain, and exquisite Christmas-tree ornaments.

⑯ **Italy.** *Moderately popular.* The main event is the architecture—a reproduction of St. Mark's Square in Venice with the Campanile (bell tower) di San Marco as its centerpiece and, behind it, the elegant and elaborately decorated Doges' Palace. Complementing these buildings are Venetian bridges, gondolas, colorful barber poles, and the sculpture of the Lion of St. Mark atop a column.

In the plaza of this pavilion you can watch and participate in a comedy show put on by an Italian theater troupe. The broad-humor farce can be amusing, but only if there is a full, lively audience. At a little shop called Il Bel Cristallo, visitors can watch artisans at work blowing crystal figurines.

⑰ **American Adventure.** *Popular.* This is a 30-minute Audio-Animatronics show about the development of the USA. The huge, Colonial-style theater features the most sophisticated and realistic Animatronics characters in Disney World. The show takes visitors from the arrival of the Pilgrims through the Revolutionary and Civil Wars, the taming of the West, the World Wars, and so on. The voyage is hosted by Benjamin Franklin and Mark Twain. Some will find the presentation a bit long, even though 30 minutes is not much time to cover 200 years of history. Many people find it inspiringly patriotic or historically skewed, but children may take this opportunity to catch a few winks—the dramatic music often puts them right to sleep.

Directly opposite the American Adventure pavilion, on the lagoon, is the open-air America Gardens Theatre, where live, high-energy, all-American shows are performed about four times a day. Show times vary but are posted each day on boards in front of the theater's entrances.

⑱ Japan. *Popular.* Elegant landscaping of rocks, streams, trees, and shrubs combines with traditional architecture to create this peaceful and charming pavilion. Inside the *torii* gates are monumental bronze sculptures of horsemen warriors and a pagoda of five levels, each of which represents one of the five elements of Buddhist belief—earth, water, fire, wind, and sky. Of special interest is the Mitsukoshi Department Store, where lacquered dinnerware, teapots, vases, bonsai trees, and Japanese dolls and toys are for sale; and the Bijutsu-kan Gallery, featuring temporary exhibits of traditional Japanese crafts such as kite-making. The Yakitori House serves inexpensive Japanese fast food in a pleasant garden—a good bet for lunch.

⑲ Morocco. *Popular.* This is one of the more spectacular-looking and exotic of the pavilions. It has a replica of the Koutoubia Minaret from a famous prayer house in Marrakesh; a gallery of Moroccan art, tapestries, and traditional costumes; and a short street with shops selling basketry, leather goods, samovars, exquisite jewelry, and an incredible assortment of metal items. Dancers move to the exotic rhythms of North Africa and get the audience in on the act.

⑳ France. *Popular.* The 18-minute film "Impressions of France" is projected on a five-panel semicircular screen and takes viewers on a romantic tour of France—through the countryside, into the Alps, along the coast, and, of course, into Paris. Viewers will experience the streets of Paris on Bastille Day, the beaches of the Riviera, the gardens of Versailles, and an ascent of the Eiffel Tower. It is a sophisticated adventure with little narration but exquisitely lyrical visuals and classical music.

The pavilion itself resembles a French boulevard lined with shops and cafes. Of special interest are Tout Pour le Gourmet, and La Maison du Vin, two shops featuring French culinary specialties, such as wines, cheeses, mustards, herbs, and pâtés. A little *patisserie/boulangerie* prepares all kinds of baked goods, and two restaurants, Bistro de Paris and Au Petit Café, are ideal for lunch. Atop this pavilion is an impressive model of the Eiffel Tower that was constructed using Alexandre-Gustave Eiffel's original blueprints.

International Gateway. This plaza, a new entrance to Epcot Center, connects the Epcot Center Resort hotels via a shop-lined boardwalk around a man-made lagoon.

㉑ United Kingdom. *Moderately popular.* On this street from Old London are a variety of architectural styles, from thatched-roof cottages to Tudor and ornate Victorian homes. The city square and rural streets are filled with numerous food, toy, and souvenir shops. The very British Rose and Crown Pub serves Stilton cheese, Bass and Guinness ales, and simple English fare. Street actors and a minstrel troupe, the "Pearly Kings and Queens," perform throughout the day, showing the same broad humor as the Italians.

㉒ Canada. *Popular.* A CircleVision film takes its audience into Canada's great outdoors, from the magnificent snow-peaked Rockies, down sprawling Arctic glaciers, across the plains to Montreal. This thoroughly engaging display makes audiences feel they are experiencing a toboggan run, a dog sled race, and the Calgary Stampede rodeo. Peaceful gardens full of roses, a rocky gorge, emporiums selling everything from sheepskins to lumberjack shirts and maple syrup, and a cafeteria-style restaurant called Le Cellier are other highlights of this quaint pavilion.

Disney-MGM Studios Theme Park

Disney-MGM Studios Theme Park sprawls under Walt Disney World's latest landmark, The Earffel Tower, a 13-story water tower capped with enormous Mickey Mouse ears. The new theme park gives visitors an opportunity to get behind the scenes and sometimes in front of the cameras at a working movie and television studio reminiscent of Hollywood in the 1930s and 1940s.

New attractions will be coming on line throughout this year. Shortly after the doors swung open in 1989, with only six attractions on 110 acres, WDW announced it would double the size of the park over the next five years, thanks to a little green frog named Kermit. Walt Disney World and Jim Henson Productions are working to bring together Kermit the Frog and Roger Rabbit. The new additions should make the park a full-day adventure.

Getting There

From Orlando, take Exit 26 off I–4 and follow the signs. From Kissimmee, stay on U.S. 192 and enter at the main Disney entrance. The Disney-MGM parking lot is about a mile up World Drive, on your right. If you are staying at a Disney hotel, *see* Getting There, at the beginning of this Chapter.

Orientation

Disney-MGM can be divided into two sections: the back-lot tour and the other attractions. Enter the park on Hollywood Boulevard, a short street lined with shops. Lockers and strollers are available at Oscar's Super Service, to the right as you enter the park. The boulevard opens onto a plaza, where the fun begins. Street actors abound and make you part of the action as you decide whether to turn right for the back-lot tour or left to the other attractions. If you want to dine at one of the two full-service restaurants—'50s Prime Time Cafe or The Hollywood Brown Derby—make reservations now even if you plan to eat off-hours.

Head to the Magic of Disney Animation and Backstage Studio Tour. Do the Animation tour first, because the lines get long and most of the artists are gone by 5. Afterward, take the back-lot tour, which can last more than two hours, depending on how much time you want to spend wandering around on your own.

Magic of Disney Animation. *Popular.* Videos of Robin Williams and Walter Cronkite teach a humorous lesson on animation. Young children may not get much out of the walk-through, in which the overhead videos explain each section, while artists, separated by soundproof glass, work beneath you. Take as much time as you want. The only drawback is that the guides are there to take you through, not to answer questions.

Backstage Studio Tour. *Very popular; all ages.* You start off with a tame but interesting tram ride past bungalows that house working crews, such as *All New Mickey Mouse Club*, into the costuming and props buildings, and out onto residential streets. See if you recognize some of the houses from television or movies. The tram then takes you to Catastrophe Canyon, where you learn about special effects by being part of them, especially if you are on the left side of the tram. The tram part of the tour ends with a quick look down a New York street.

Roger Rabbit's purple paw a prints will direct you through the Loony Bin. Boxes of props lining the corridor will entertain kids on their way out. The Studio Catering Co. is here, too, and it is a good place to eat your lunch if you brought one. They do serve sandwiches and drinks, and it beats waiting for restaurants in the park, unless you don't want to miss the nifty themed eateries. You are on your own to explore the city streets and to see if a production is being filmed.

Walk over to the special effects water tank, but plan ahead which row you want to get in. There is a reason the first floor is wet. From there you'll follow a tour guide to an indoor special-effects workshop and shooting stage, followed by a soundstage and a postproduction and sound effects area. Volunteers can participate at many of the stops. You'll wind up the tour previewing a soon-to-be-released film. Although the information is fascinating and often presented by stars via video or by peering over the shoulders of Disney technicians at work, the tour keeps moving, allowing for little opportunity to ask questions or linger.

The Great Movie Ride. *Very popular; all ages.* Housed in a re-creation of Grauman's Chinese Theater, this ride has you and your guide interacting with the Audio-Animatronics cast as you glide by scenes from *Singin' in the Rain, Casablanca, Alien,* and other memorable movie moments.

Epic Stunt Spectacular. *Very popular; all ages.* Don't let the long lines deter you here. A 2,000-seat amphitheater wipes these lines out quickly. With the help of a dozen volunteers from the audience, stuntmen re-create scenes from *Raiders of the Lost Ark,* including an exploding airplane, actors falling off fortress walls, and an overturning truck. Stunts are demonstrated and explained. Volunteers, who perform as extras, are safe, but the stunts are all for real, and the stars occasionally have been injured.

The Monster Sound Show. *Popular; all ages.* Chevy Chase and Martin Short star in a comic-thriller film, complete with predictable sound effects. At a second showing, volunteer audio artists from the audience try to re-create the sounds. The third viewing is with the amateur artists' own sound effects. As you leave the film, don't rush through SoundWorks in the next room. Take some time to try some of the hands-on activities, and be sure to enter Soundsations.

SuperStar Television. *Popular; all ages.* Volunteers are put in television roles as the studio audience is cued with "applause" cards. On stage all you see are the amateur actors with their directors and cameramen, but if you look up at one of the eight large screens, you will see these actors performing with the likes of Lucille Ball, Ed Sullivan, and Johnny Carson. Actors are chosen from the line waiting to get into the 1,000-seat theater. Even if you don't get selected, the cameras pan the audience, so you still might be on television. Keep your eyes on the screens.

Star Tours. *Very popular; all ages.* A warning outside this ride says you shouldn't have back problems, a heart condition, get motion sickness easily, or have other physical limitations. Pregnant women and children under age 3 are not allowed on the ride, and children under age 7 must be accompanied by an adult. This is a simulated flight to the Moon of Endor from *Return of the Jedi.* Like Body Wars in Epcot, you are placed in a 40-seat simulator, as you are sent rocketing through an astroidlike field of ice to battle with an Imperial Star Destoyer before evading blasts from the Death Star.

Here Come the Muppets. *Very popular; all ages.* Kermit acts as host as his buddies, including Miss Piggy, Fozzy Bear, and Gonzo, entertain you and remind you of the genius of the late Jim Henson. New this year will be a 3-D movie starring the Muppets.

"Let's Make a Deal." *Popular; all ages.* Monty Hall came back to breathe new life into this old game show, which is taped at the Disney-MGM Studios between 11 and 5. Park guests can be contestants or members of the studio audience. Call 560–8225. When the show isn't taping for television, guests can still play Let's Make a Deal. The show is taped and then sold. Check for showtimes at Soundstage 1 in the Studio Backlot or at the Production and Information Window at the Main Entrance.

Honey, I Shrunk the Kids. New playground for kids in which they enter a backyard where the blades of grass are 30 feet high and the ants are gigantic.

Also new: **Dick Tracy Starring in Diamond Double Cross,** a musical song-and-dance performance Wednesday–Monday at the Theater of the Stars; and **Teenage Mutant Ninja Turtles,** who perform daily behind the Chinese Theatre.

On the drawing boards: **Noah's Ark,** a nighttime show by Andrew Lloyd Webber, to be presented on the waterway linking Epcot and Disney-MGM, perhaps by the end of 1992.

Time Out The restaurants are more memorable than the food, but if you want to be served, reservations should be made early, unless you want to snack your way through the park on hot dogs, popcorn, and ice cream. If you are staying at a Disney hotel or one on the property, you can call one or two days ahead to the only two restaurants that take reservations, **'50s Prime Time Cafe** and **The Hollywood Brown Derby.** Call 407/828–4000 between noon and 9 PM or, if you are at a Lake Buena Vista Village hotel, call 407/824–8800. You cannot make reservations for the same day that you call.

Other Attractions in Walt Disney World

Typhoon Lagoon. This 50-acre aquatic entertainment complex features the largest waterslide mountain in the world. The mountain is just under 100 feet high, with nine waterslides shooting down it into white-water rivers and swirling pools. There are huge wave-making lagoons for swimming and surfing.

The water park also includes a Swiss Family Robinson–type tropical island covered with lush greenery, where guests can play at being shipwrecked. A saltwater pool contains a coral reef where snorkelers come mask-to-face with all sorts of Caribbean sea creatures, such as groupers, parrotfish, and even baby sharks. *Typhoon Lagoon, tel. 407/560–4142. Admission: $18.25 adults one day, $16.25 resort guests; $14.50/$13 children one day. Open 9:30–4:30, longer in the summer.*

River Country. In the backwoods setting of the Fort Wilderness Campground Resort, kids can slide, splash, and swim about in an aquatic playground, complete with whitewater inner-tubing channels and corkscrew waterslides that splash down into a 300,000-gallon pond. The pool is heated during the winter so kids can take a dip here all year round. The lake, with its waterslides, is too chilly for most swimmers during the winter. In the summer, River Country can get very congested, so it's best to come first thing in the morning. *Fort Wilderness Resort, tel. 407/824–2760. Admission: $11.75 adults one day, $10.75 resort guests, $10.50 Magic Kingdom Card; $17.75/$16.75/$16.50 two days; $9.25/$8.25/$8 children 3–9 one day, $13.75/$12.75/$12.50 two days. Open 10–5, longer in the summer.*

Discovery Island. Covered with exotic flora, small, furry animals, and colorful birdlife, this little island makes a great escape from the man-made tourist attractions of Disney World. Visitors listen to nature as they stroll along winding pathways, across footbridges, and through one of the biggest aviaries in the United States. Disney did not create these creatures—he just brought them here. Keep an eye out for the Galapagos tortoises, trumpeter swans, scarlet ibis, and bald eagles. It takes less than an hour to walk the trails and see the exhibits, but many visitors stay longer, luxuriating in this respite from the lines and orchestrated activities on the mainland.

Tickets are sold at Fort Wilderness' River Country (just outside the gates of the Magic Kingdom near the turnstiles), at the TTC, at guest service desks in the Disney resorts, and on the island itself. You can get there by watercraft from the Magic Kingdom, Contemporary Resorts, Polynesian Village, Grand Floridian, and River Country in Fort Wilderness. *Discovery Island, tel. 407/824–2875. Admission: $8 adults; $4.50 children 3–9. Open 10-5, longer in summer. River Country/ Discovery Island combination ticket: $15 adults one day, $14 resort guests, $13.75 Magic Kingdom Card; $11/$10/$9.75, children 3–9.*

4 Exploring Outside Walt Disney World

If you feel that you have done all there is to do in Disney World or that you and Mickey need a short vacation from each other, don't despair; there is plenty more to do around Orlando. What you'll discover is that many attractions outside the walls of the Magic Kingdom are equally enjoyable and often less crowded and less expensive.

The Major Attractions Section includes theme parks and other attractions that singularly will require the better part of your day to visit. The Day Trips section is a suggested itinerary of smaller attractions that, visited together, make for an enjoyable day's jaunt. General directions are offered here, but it is advised that you call in advance for more specific directions tailored to your own itinerary.

Major Attractions

Numbers in the margin correspond with points of interest on the Major Attractions map.

❶ **Spirit Country.** For a totally different sort of experience, head about 35 miles north of Orlando to the town of Cassadaga, which possesses one of the nation's largest communities of psychic mediums. These mediums communicate with your spirits and the spirits of others primarily for purposes of "healing" a sickness of the soul. They believe in communication with the dead and assert that supernatural experiences such as clairvoyance, levitation, and materialization are functions of everlasting spirits.

The Cassadaga Spiritualist Camp welcomes visitors who wish either to sit in on one of the unusual Sunday church services (usually held from 10:30 to 11:30 AM) or to get a "reading" from one of the camp members. You are expected to find a medium who is right for you by walking or driving through this rustic, five-by-five-block neighborhood and stopping at the house that seems to be giving off the right sort of energy.

Whatever your belief, it is worth a trip here if only to walk around the serene, wooded camp, attend a church service, and learn more about spiritualism from the materials at the Southern Cassadaga Bookstore at 1112 Stevens Street (open Mon.– Sat. 9:30–5, Sun. noon–4), or from talking to some of the mediums. The people here are friendly and wholesome; all they ask of visitors is that they dress appropriately and treat the site with respect (in other words, don't litter). *Cassadaga Spiritualist Camp, Box 319, Cassadaga 32706, tel. 904/228–2880. Cassadaga is about 35 mi northeast of Orlando. To get there, take I–4 to Exit 54 for Lake Helen and Cassadaga.*

❷ **Universal Studios Florida.** The largest motion picture and television studio outside of Hollywood makes learning fun. Learn about production by viewing—or possibly being a part of— *Nickelodeon;* get a lesson about animation by riding along with Yogi Bear, the Flintstones, and some of their friends; discover the secrets of special effects by seeing how it was done in *Ghostbusters* and other movie-themed attractions, most of which had a helping hand from Universal's creative consultant Steven Spielberg:

Back to the Future. Doc Brown sends you through time where you will see dinosaurs; the Wright brothers at Kitty Hawk,

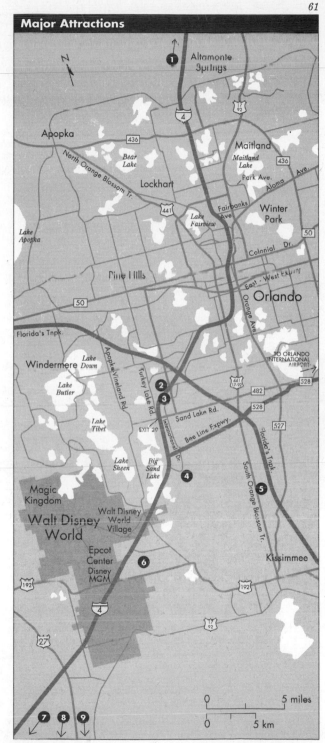

Major Attractions

NC; Leonardo da Vinci in Venice, Italy; and a harrowing incident at Niagara Falls. It is all done with the help of a seven-story Omni-Max surrounding screen, flight simulators, and wild special effects.

Earthquake—The Big One. You are on a rapid transit train in San Francisco when you find out what an earthquake measuring 8.3 on the Richter Scale is all about, including fire and flood.

E.T.'s Adventure. You saw Elliot save E.T. in the movies, now it's your turn to help him. His planet is in peril, and he has come to Earth for help. On your bike ride across the moon you will feel the wind on your face and pedal through purple fog. E.T. will thank you personally. (How he knows your name is a trade secret that Universal won't reveal.)

Jaws. In an attraction with this name, you know you will see the three-ton, 24-foot killer shark as you depart on a pontoon ride. Yes, he attacks the boat, and this critter is relentless.

King Kong Kongfrontation. King Kong goes berserk while you are riding the Roosevelt Island tram. Your confrontation with him is so up close and personal, you will actually smell banana breath before he hurls your tram car. Frightening? Check the video replay for your reactions.

Equally as entertaining, but without the bone-jarring experiences, are the production presentations that demonstrate mixing, set design, sound effects, dubbing, costuming, editing, and special effects. In **Alfred Hitchcock: The Art of Making Movies,** you'll experience memorable scenes from some of his suspense classics. **Ghostbusters: A Live-Action Spooktacular** combines live action with modern cinema technology as a demonstration of special effects. **Screen Test Adventure Studio** makes you the star in your own film. You get top billing and a video of your film debut to take home. **The Funtastic World of Hanna-Barbera** allows you to participate in an animation adventure as you ride along during a high-speed chase. After the dust settles, you will get a lesson on animation, and then an opportunity to put it to use. **Phantom of the Opera Horror Make-Up Show** is a lesson in the secrets of movie makeup. Lassie, Benji, Einstein from *Back to the Future*, and an assortment of horses, cats, and pigeons, with their trainers, demonstrate animal acting skills in **Animal Actors Stage.** You get to be executive producer in an episode of "Murder, She Wrote" in the **Murder, She Wrote Post-Production Theater.**

Because each shop and restaurant is set up to be used for a shoot, the entire 444 acres feel like a back lot. A walking tour takes you to more than 50 locations, ranging from Angkor-Wat to a New York street.

There is always a show in production at the **Nickelodeon Production Center.** Contact guest services about children's auditions. *1000 Universal Studios Plaza, Orlando 32819, tel. 407/363-8000. Admission: $29 adults one day, $49 two days; $23 children 3–11 one day, $39 two days. Open daily 9–7, extended hours in the summer and holidays. To get there, get off I–4 at Exit 29 and follow the signs, or take Exit 30B and go north on Kirkman Road. Follow the signs. Parking $3. Nominal charge for kennels.*

❸ **Wet 'n Wild.** Nothing's better on a hot, sticky, summer day than a cooling dive in the ocean. Unfortunately, the coast is at least a

30-minute drive away, so if you're in a hurry, head to Wet 'n Wild—an aquatic amusement park where you can swim, slide, and play water sports until you shrivel up into a prune. It's conveniently located, just off International Drive. The water slides are better than in River Country, but the environment—a big concrete pool—leaves much to be desired.

The park has over 14 different state-of-the-art water rides, some appealing strictly to children, others to the whole family, and yet others to slide-crazed daredevils. You don't have to know how to swim to enjoy the action because the water depth never exceeds standing height, and there are plenty of brawny, certified lifeguards on duty.

The park has its fair share of snack stands, but visitors are allowed to bring their own food and picnic around the pool or on the lakeside beach. *6200 International Dr. (at Republic Dr.), Orlando, tel. 407/351–WILD or 800/992–WILD. Admission: $17.95, two-day pass $26.90 adults; $15.95, two-day pass $23.90 children 3–12. Half-price discounts begin at 3 PM, 5 PM in summer. Hours vary, but generally 9 AM–11 PM in the summer and 10 AM–5 PM in the spring and fall. Closed Jan.–mid-Feb. AE, MC, V.*

4 **Sea World.** You may have come to Orlando for Disney World, but it would be goofy not to visit Sea World while you are here. It is the world's largest zoological park, an aquatic wonderland filled with an ocean's worth of sea creatures that perform for you, or that you can pet or simply watch. If you plan your tour of the shows and exhibits when you arrive, you should be able to see most of the park in about six hours (in time perhaps for some afternoon golf). Of course, you may also want to spend a full day at a more leisurely pace. Organize your visit around the times of the shows, not by the areas they are in. The park is much smaller than it seems on a map and, as you will soon discover, the exhibits are no more than a few minutes' walk from each other. Ask the staff for directions: It can save lots of time. Don't think that, as in Disney World, you will need a week-long pass to see everything here. One day, and an evening if you plan to see the evening shows, is enough. To get a quick overview of the park and the surrounding landscape take a ride up the 400-foot Sky Tower. *Admission to Sky Tower: $2.50.*

A far cry from the little mouse who lives down the road, the mascot of Sea World is a few thousand pounds of affectionate, carnivorous killer whale. Shamu is the most popular feature of the park. She will be joined this year by Baby Namu, who was born in 1989, the third killer whale born at Sea World. The tank that the whales swim in with their parents, aunts, and uncles may seem small, but actually is filled with more than 5 million gallons of salt water—give or take a few hundred gallons that have splashed on the onlookers by the end of each show. Shamu impresses her fans with jumps, twists, squirts, and kisses in "Shamu: New Visions" narrated by James Earl Jones, but be careful not to sit in the first 10 rows of the stadium, especially if you are carrying a camera, unless you enjoy getting drenched.

The two other most entertaining shows are "New Friends," starring whales and dolphins, and "Clyde and Seamore 10,000 BC," starring a walrus and an otter. These are the funniest, corniest routines in Sea World and are not to be missed.

"Penguin Encounter," featuring more than 200 formally attired aquatic clowns who splash, swim, dive, and gobble fish in a habitat aquarium, is as entertaining as it is informative. The show gets very crowded midday, so try to go in the morning or late afternoon.

Sea World's most elaborate exhibit is the shark tank, where visitors learn about the life cycle and habits of these ravenous creatures. By the end of your educational, 40-minute underwater tunnel tour, you may even begin to think of these man-eating creatures as friends. "Shark Encounter," a film of a shark's feeding frenzy, is chilling. If you want to spend more time watching the sharks, re-enter the building through the door to your right.

If you feel like chumming up to a few sea creatures, buy a few boxes of herring and feed the dolphins, seals, sea lions, and sting rays in their feeding pools. Drop fish in their mouths as they playfully swim or leap past you. These feeding pools can be the most emotionally rewarding of all the exhibits.

Other presentations include a multimedia show in Sea World Theatre—a cool retreat in the heat of the day. "Window to the Sea" includes an interview on animal training, an ocean voyage looking for sharks, and a journey aboard a research submarine. Another popular event is the USO Water Ski Show, where teams of world-class water skiers perform acrobatics while skimming the water at high speed. Parents can relax at Cap'n Kids' World while the kids climb aboard, under, around, and through a 55-foot pirate ship and shoot water cannons at each other.

Every evening Sea World puts on a Polynesian Luau, a dinner show featuring hula dancers, drum music, fire jugglers, and other acts from the islands of the South Pacific. Shamu, the sea lions, and the otters have special night performances, with a grand finale of fireworks and laser show. An alternative to the luau is a dinner of alligator meat or some less exotic fare at the Al E. Gator's Key West Eatery.

7007 Sea World Dr., Orlando 32821, tel. 407/351–3600, in FL, 800/432–1178, outside FL, 800/327–2424. Open year-round, 9 AM–8 PM with extended hours in the summer. Call for details. Admission: $25.50 adults (weekly pass $28.95); $21.70 children 3–9 (weekly pass $24.95); Polynesian Luau Dinner and Show, 6:45 nightly, $27.95 adults; $18.95 children 8–12; $9.95 children 3–7. Luau reservations tel. in FL, 800/227–8048, outside FL, 800/327–2424. To get there, take I–4 to the Beeline Expressway exit and drive 1 mi to the Sea World/International Dr. exit. Go to the first traffic light, make a left, and follow signs to one of the parking lots. Parking and dog kennels are free.

⑤ Gatorland Zoo. This is an unusual attraction that features over 400 alligators and 40 crocodiles swimming and basking in the sun in a swampy lake. There's also a nursery with thousands of alligators crawling all over each other and a zoo that houses many other reptiles, in addition to monkeys, farm animals, and even a tapir.

A boardwalk with a swinging suspension bridge takes you through a cypress swamp, where you can view wildlife in its natural environment. Don't miss the Gator Jumparoo (performed four times daily); gators leap out of the water to sink their teeth into a chicken dangling four feet overhead. The best jumparoo is the first one in the morning, about 10:30, when the beasts are hungriest. *14501 S. Orange Blossom Trail, tel. 407/ 855–5496. Admission: $7.95 adults, $4.95 children 3–11. Open daily 8–6; June–Aug. 8–8.*

❻ Water Mania. Conveniently located among the inexpensive hotels on U.S. 192 and across from Old Town, this park has all the requisite rides and slides, including a new flume. It also has a popular maze, miniature golf, a sandy beach, a picnic area, snack bars, and gift shops. Concerts are sometimes held here, and you can enjoy the entertainment while floating in inner tubes. *6073 W. Irlo Bronson Memorial Hwy. (U.S. 192), Kissimmee 34746, tel. 800/527–3092, or in Orlando, 407/239– 8448, or in Kissimmee, 407/396–2626 in Kissimmee. Admission: $16.95 adults, $14.95 children 3–12. Open Mar.–May, daily 10–5; June–Aug., daily 9–9; Sept.–Nov., daily 10–5; closed Dec.–Feb.*

❼ Cypress Gardens. A visitor can only imagine how glorious and dignified Cypress Gardens must have looked before it was converted into the glitzy amusement playground that it is today. Commercial or not, however, it is still an exceptionally beautiful place. Cypress Gardens is Central Florida's oldest continuously running attraction (yes, even older than Disney World). It was founded as a public botanical garden during the Depression by Dick and Julie Pope. In World War II, when her husband was off serving his country and visitors were few, Julie attracted patrons by dressing the women on her staff in antebellum-style wide hoop skirts and placing them in strategic locations around the gardens. Visitors were so enchanted that these "Flowers of the South" became a tradition as important to the gardens as the tropical blooms themselves.

The gardens are filled with some 8,000 varieties of plants and flowers, which bloom year round, tended by a staff of more than 50 horticulturists. While relaxing under the shade of a massive banyan tree you can gaze into a world of tropical and subtropical flora. On the opposite side of the gardens are birds, mammals, and reptiles from all over the globe. There are live alligator shows, a parrot show, and such exotic animals as lemurs, emus, and dromedaries. Children can touch white-tail deer, tortoises, and other tame creatures.

In addition to the flora and fauna are several other attractions, including an Ice Palace skating show that children tend to enjoy more than adults. At the Aquacade pool, high divers and synchronized swimmers demonstrate their skills. The biggest event at the gardens is the water-skiing show, a 30-minute revue of high-speed stunts along the shores of Lake Eloise. Don't forget to bring your camera: Cypress Gardens is really a strikingly beautiful place. And don't miss the fireworks and laser light show during extended hours at certain times of the year. *Box 1, Cypress Gardens 33884, tel. 813/324–2111, in FL, 800/ 282–2123, outside FL, 800/237–4826. Admission: $18.95 adults, $12.95 children 3–9. Open daily 9–6. To get there, take I–4 west to the U.S. 27 south exit. Follow signs to Winter Haven. When you reach Waverly, turn right (west) on Rte. 540 and drive about 5 mi to the Gardens entrance. It is about a 45-minute drive from Disney World.*

⑧ Bok Tower Gardens. If Cypress Gardens whets your appetite for natural beauty, drive some 20 minutes farther south and enjoy a forest full of plants, flowers, trees, and wildlife native to subtropical Florida.

Bok Tower Gardens is a sanctuary that was designed in 1928 by Frederick Law Olmsted, Jr., son of the famous planner of New York's Central Park. The park was dedicated by President Calvin Coolidge in 1929 to the American people on behalf of Edward Bok, an immigrant from the Netherlands who became a successful New York writer and editor. Shady paths meander through pine forests on a hillside that rises 324 feet above sea level, Florida's highest measured point of land. At the crest of this hill is the 200-foot Bok Singing Tower, made of pink and gray marble covered with intricate latticework. Bronze doors are covered with reliefs of Biblical scenes, and pink and turquoise mosaics depict Florida's exotic wildlife. The tower is a carillon with 53 bronze bells that ring every half-hour. Each day at 3 PM there is a 45-minute recital; depending on when you are there, you may hear Early American folk songs, Appalachian tunes, Irish ballads, Latin hymns, and so on. There are also moonlight recitals and special programs with visiting artists. This world of silvery moats, mockingbirds and swans, blooming thickets, and hidden sundials will be a welcome retreat from the land of highways, malls, and amusement parks. *Box 3810, Lake Wales, 33853, tel. 813/676–1408. Admission: $3 adults, children under 12 free. Open daily 8–5. To get there, continue past the Cypress Gardens turnoff on U.S. 27 for about 5 mi, turn off on Rte. 17A to Alt. U.S. 27. Follow signs past the orange groves, through the town of Lake Wales, to the park.*

⑨ Busch Gardens. If you have seen all of Orlando's amusement parks and are still looking for more action, Busch Gardens, only a 75-minute drive from Disney World, is a "must see." It is the third most popular tourist attraction in the entire state, and for good reason. It is an imaginatively and convincingly designed turn-of-the-century African theme park for more than 3,000 animals, with an emphasis on breeding endangered species and creating natural habitats.

The Moroccan-style architecture alone is worth a visit. Huts, tents, and bazaars filled with imported goods make visitors feel they have stumbled onto an African stage set. The stadium where the Sea World-type "Dolphins of the Deep" show is presented is inspired by the traditional architecture of Timbuktu.

Although there are many things to see and do, the park's real draw is its animals. There is an extensive children's petting zoo and habitat displays for all sorts of animals. Tigers pace a tropical island, crocodiles bask in swamps, elephants spray themselves in a rocky cave, and antelopes, zebras, camels, and countless other quadrupeds graze on 60 acres of savannah.

One of the most fascinating attractions is the World of Birds. This is the most impressive bird show in Florida and should not be missed. Birds you can see up close include a bald eagle and a golden eagle—two of the most noble creatures on earth; countless owls, vultures, and parrots; and a condor so big that it is kept on a leash.

After you've seen the animals, take a tour through the Budweiser brewery (an Anheuser-Busch brewery). Or take a few spins on the two teeth-clenching, corkscrew roller coast-ers, or a dip on the new Tanganyika Tidal Wave, a water slide with a 55-foot drop. Busch Gardens may be a significant drive from Orlando, but few visitors regret the trip. *3000 E. Busch Blvd. at 40th St., Tampa, tel. 813/971–8282. Admission: $23.95. Parking $2. Open daily 9:30–6. Extended hours during the summer and selected holidays; phone for details. To get there, take I–4 west to Tampa and exit at I–75. Take Exit 54 and follow signs to the park.*

Day Trips

Numbers in the margin correspond with points of interest on the Day Trips map.

Park Avenue A drive to trendy Park Avenue in Orlando is a good way to start
1 your day. The **scenic boat tour** of Winter Park is a relaxing, hour-long 12-mile cruise that sails past large lakeside homes and a different view of Rollins College. *Scenic boat tour of Winter Park, 312 Morse Blvd., Winter Park 32789, tel. 407/644–4056. Admission: $5 adults, $2.50 children 2–11; group rates available. Open daily 10–4; closed Christmas. From International Dr. take I–4 east through town to Fairbanks Ave. exit. Turn right and follow to the traffic light at Park Ave. (Rollins College is on the right). Turn left on Park Ave., then right on Morse Blvd. Take Morse Blvd. to the dock at the end.*

2 Just off Park Avenue is the **Charles Hosmer Morse Museum of American Art,** which features an outstanding collection of stained-glass windows and other decorative arts by Louis Tiffany (son of Charles Tiffany of New York jewelry fame). *133 E. Welbourne Ave., tel. 407/645–5311. Admission: $2.50 adults, $1 students and children. Open Tues.–Sat. 9:30–4, Sun. 1–4.*

At the south end of Park Avenue is the lakeside campus of Rollins College. Take time to look at the Spanish-style architec-
3 ture. Also on campus is the **Cornell Fine Arts Center,** which exhibits 19th-century American paintings from the West, as well as a few older European works. *Tel. 407/646–2526. Admission free. Open Tues.–Fri. 10–5, weekends 1–5.*

Loch Haven Area Orlando's **Loch Haven Park** houses a complex featuring his-
4 torical, artistic, and scientific exhibits. Take I–4 to Exit 43 (Princeton St.) and travel east for about a mile to the park. Of interest in the **Orlando Science Center** are science exhibits, the John Young Planetarium with weekend evening cosmic concerts, a Foucault pendulum, and hands-on displays. *810 Rollins St., Orlando 32803, tel. 407/896–7151. Admission: $4 adults, $3 children 4–17, $10 family. Open Mon.–Thurs. 9–5, Fri. 9–9, Sat. noon–9, Sun. noon–5.*

In the same building is the **Orange County Historical Museum,** which has exhibits on Orlando's early years and the growth of its orange industry. *Tel. 407/898–8320. Admission: $2 adults, $1 children 4–17.*

Also in the complex is the **Orlando Museum of Art,** with a collection of pre-Columbian artworks and 19th- and 20th-century paintings. Call for information on special exhibits. *Tel. 407/896–4231. Admission: $3 adults, $2 children 6–18. Open Tues.–Thurs. 9–5, Fri. 9–7:30, Sat. 10–5, Sun. noon–5.*

5 For a pleasant respite from the Florida heat, visit **Leu Gardens**—a 56-acre display of rose gardens, a 50-foot floral clock,

Charles Hosmer Morse
Museum of American
Art, **2**

Cornell Fine Arts
Center, **3**

Elvis Presley
Museum, **7**

Florida Citrus
Tower, **11**

Flying Tigers Warbird
Air Museum, **10**

Lakeridge Winery, **12**

Leu Gardens, **5**

Loch Haven Park, **4**

Mystery Fun House, **6**

Pirates Cove
Adventure Golf, **8**

Scenic Boat Tour, **1**

Tupperware World
Headquarters, **9**

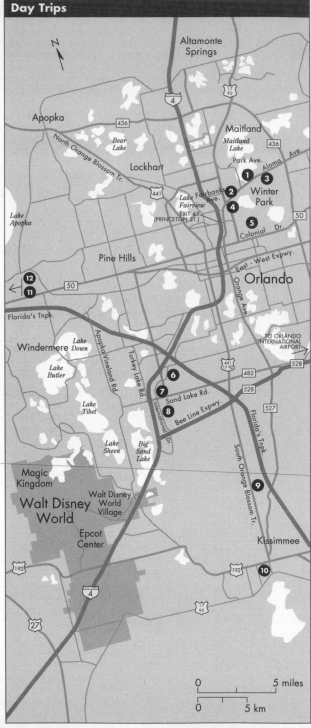

Day Trips

and the largest camellia collection in eastern North America (in bloom October–March). You can also tour the 19th-century mansion on the grounds. *1730 N. Forest Ave., Orlando 32803, tel. 407/849-2820. Admission: $2 adults, $1 children 6–16. Gardens open daily 9–5, closed Christmas; house open Tues.– Sat. 10–3:30, Sun. and Mon. 1–3:30. Get off I–4 at Exit 43 (Princeton St.), drive east to end. Turn right on Mills Ave. Turn left on Nebraska and continue to garden entrance on Forest Ave.*

International Drive
6

To occupy the kids, International Drive has a number of small attractions. Check out **Mystery Fun House,** with its mirror maze, video arcade, miniature golf, and a laser game. *5767 Major Blvd., Orlando 32819, tel. 407/351-3355. Admission to complex: $7.95; admission free to video arcade; admission to Starbase Omega (laser game): $5.95. Open daily 10 AM–11 PM, box office closed at 10 PM.*

7

Farther south on International Drive is the **Elvis Presley Museum,** in Dowdy Plaza (at the intersection of International and Carrier drives). There are more than 200 items associated with the King, including one of his motorcycles, his 1977 Lincoln Continental, photographs, jewelry, and other memorabilia. *7200 International Dr. (Dowdy Plaza), Orlando 32819, tel. 407/345-9427. Admission: $4 adults, $3 children 7–12. Open daily 9 AM–10 PM.*

8

After a refreshment from Mercado Mediterranean Village (*see* Chapter 5), cross the street to **Pirate's Cove Adventure Golf,** with two 18-hole miniature golf courses winding up mountains, through caves, and over waterfalls. *8601 International Dr., Orlando 32819, tel. 407/352-7378. Admission: $9 for 18 holes, $10 all day adults; $8 for 18 holes, $9 all day children 12 and under. Open daily 9 AM–11:30 PM.*

U.S. 441 and
U.S. 192
9

A drive down U.S. 441 and across U.S. 192 could include gators, Tupperware, World War II aircraft, and a big splash. You can begin at **Gatorland Zoo** (*see* Major Attractions, above). Take I–4 to the Beeline Expressway and exit south on U.S. 441. After Gatorland, continue south for less than a mile to **Tupperware World Headquarters.** Free 25-minute tours are given, but sorry—no free samples. *U.S. 441, Box 2353, Orlando 32802, tel. 407/847-3111. Open weekdays 9–4. Tours every 15 min.*

10

Continue south to U.S. 441 and then U.S. 192 (Irlo Bronson Memorial Highway). Turn right. Travel on U.S. 192 past the entrance to the Kissimmee Airport, and turn left onto Hoagland Boulevard (Airport Road). Here is the **Flying Tigers Warbird Air Museum,** an aircraft restoration facility known as Bombertown USA. Recently turned into a museum of World War II planes, it has hands-on displays, personnel to answer questions, and a gift shop. You can finish the day by cooling off at Water Mania (*see* Major Attractions, above), a few miles west on U.S. 192. *231 Hoagland Blvd., Kissimmee 32741, tel. 407/933-1942. Admission: $5 adults, $4 senior citizens and children under 4. Open weekdays 8–8, Sat. 9–8, Sun. 9–6.*

Lake County
11

To see Florida from a different perspective, drive to the **Florida Citrus Tower** in Lake County. The tower is said to be the highest observation point in the state. Grove tours are offered, and you can also visit citrus candy and marmalade factories, a citrus packing plant, glassblower's workshop, ice cream parlor, restaurant, and gift shop. From the Florida Citrus Tower, head ⑫ north on U.S. 27 to the **Lakeridge Winery** (entrance on the left). The winery is known for its blanc du bois and Suwannee; take a free tour and try some wine. There is also an audiovisual presentation and a gift shop. *Florida Citrus Tower is on U.S. 27 in Clermont, 1 mi north of Rte. 50, about 45 min west of Orlando. Tel. 904/394–8585. Admission to tower: $3 adults, $2 children 10–15. Open daily 8–6. From the Citrus Tower, continue north on U.S. 27 a few miles to Lakeridge. Tel. 904/394–8627 or 800/ 476–VINE. Open Mon.–Sat. 10–6, Sun. noon–6.*

Cruises

If you are interested in taking a cruise while in Florida, either for six hours or six days, there are plenty to choose from. Destinations range from the vast Atlantic Ocean to the islands of the Bahamas. For more information *see* Cruises in Before You Go in Chapter 1, Essential Information.

5 Shopping

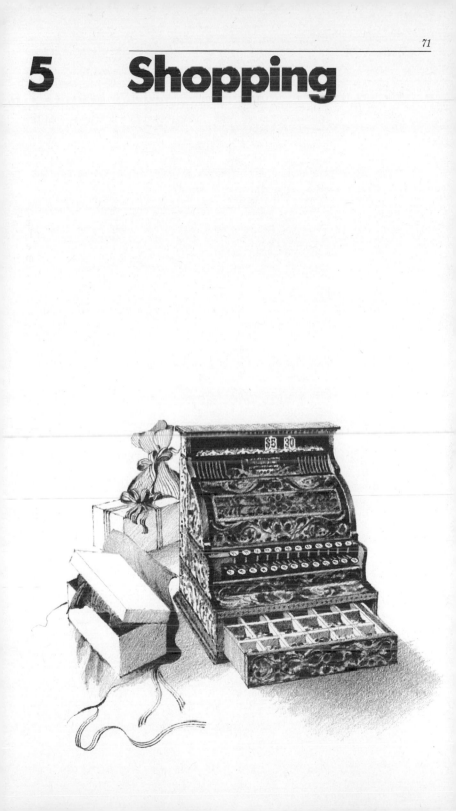

Shopping is part of the entertainment at Walt Disney World. There's something in every price range in virtually every store, so even kids on allowances can get in on the act. For details about special-interest shops in Epcot's World Showcase *see* Exploring Walt Disney World in Chapter 3. What follows is a look at other unique shops at the Disney parks and throughout the greater Orlando area.

Orlando is packed with malls. They are everywhere. It is virtually impossible to step outside your hotel room without seeing a mall or a sign advertising one. You'll find everything from shopping complexes to flea markets, factory outlets, specialty stores, department stores, and gift shops. The area provides a great opportunity to do a lifetime of shopping in a few days.

Almost all malls and outlets are open Monday to Saturday from 9 to 7 and on Sunday from 11 to 7. Most stores accept traveler's checks and major credit cards.

Walt Disney World

You'll be able to find Disney trinkets in every park, but there are a few shops throughout the property that carry unique items, like Magic Kingdom's Frontier Trading Post, where you can find western-style gifts.

Disney-MGM Studios Theme Park Be sure to check out **Sid Cahuenga's One-of-a-Kind,** to the left as you enter the park. Alongside old movie posters and autographed pictures are original costumes once worn by stars in feature movies. The **Animation Gallery,** at the end of the Animation Tour, sells original Disney animation cels, books, collectibles, and exclusive limited-edition reproductions.

Epcot Center Although the real shopping here is done at the pavilions in World Showcase, the best place for souvenirs is on the way out at Future World's **Centorium** in Communicore East. It has the largest selection of Epcot goodies.

Magic Kingdom Inside Cinderella Castle is **The King's Gallery,** where you can buy imported European clocks, chess sets, and tapestries, while artisans perform intricate metalwork. Another nifty nook is **Harmony Barber Shop,** on the west side of Main Street, where they sell old-time shaving items like mustache cups. This will just whet your appetite for **Olde World Antiques** in Frontierland, where you can find expensive antique jewelry, hutches, pewter, and brass. To get monogrammed mouse ears, stop at **The Chapeau,** on the east side of Main Street, which is extremely crowded at the end of the evening; you can also go to **The Mad Hatter,** in Fantasyland.

Factory Outlet Malls

The International Drive area is lined with factory outlet stores, most of them on the northeast end. These outlets are clumped together in expansive malls or scattered along the Drive. Much of the merchandise is discounted from 20% to 75%. You can find just about anything, some of it top quality. But be advised, these are not charming places to shop. Most of you will want to make your purchases and continue on your way.

Belz Factory Outlet Mall and Annexes. This is the largest collection of outlet stores—nearly 100—located in a mall and in three nearby annexes. The atmosphere is "bargain basement," but it's possible to come away with some good buys. Outlets include Danskin, London Fog, Bally Shoes, Bass Shoes, Anne Klein, Carole Hochman (featuring Christian Dior), Van Heusen, Big R (featuring Rawlings sporting goods), Fieldcrest/Cannon, Mikasa, Polly Flinders, Oshkosh, and Calvin Klein. *5401 W. Oakridge Rd., Orlando (at the northern tip of International Dr.), tel. 407/352–9600. Open Mon.–Sat. 10–9, Sun. 10–6.*

Quality Outlet Center and Quality Center East. These are two interconnected malls with 23 brand-name factory outlet stores including American Tourister, Great Western Boots, Corning/ Revereware, Royal Doulton, Villeroy & Boch, and Mikasa. *5409 and 5529 International Dr. (1 block north of Kirkman Rd.), tel. 407/423–5885.*

Denim World. A great place for Levi's, Lee, Activewear, and so on, always on sale. Often two-for-one deals, as well. You may have a hard time finding your size, but there are free alterations while you wait. Bring a book and you may just finish it. *7623 International Dr., tel. 407/351–5704.*

Edwin Watts Golf Shop. A no-handicap shop for golfing equipment. *7297 Turkey Lake Rd., tel. 407/345–8451.*

Dansk Factory Outlet. All the dinnerware, flatware, glassware, cookware you can imagine—and all at discount prices. *7000 International Dr., tel. 407/351–2425.*

Flea Markets

When you see signs for flea markets, remember that most are nothing but collections of shops run by small-time retailers. Bargains are possible on all sorts of bric-a-brac.

Flea World. It claims to be America's largest flea market under one roof. It just might be! With more than 1,500 booths, there is plenty here that you may want, but only after wading through piles of junk. You can find everything from samurai swords to costume jewelry, as well as a zoo. *30 minutes north of Orlando (I–4 to Exit 50, east to Hwy. 17–92, then right 1 mi), tel. 407/645–1792. Open Fri.–Sun., rain or shine, 8–5.*

Malls/Department Stores

National department stores are scattered throughout the city, but two large malls in particular are likely to carry whatever you are looking for.

The Florida Mall. This shopping complex includes Sears, J.C. Penney's, Belk Lindsey, Maison Blanche, 167 specialty shops, theaters, and one of the better food courts around. The **Florida Mall Terrace** is next door with J. Byron's, Phar-Mor, Service Merchandise, and more. *8001 S. Orange Blossom Trail, Orlando (4½ miles east of I–4 and International Dr.), tel. 407/851–6255.*

Altamonte Mall. The largest mall in Central Florida was renovated in 1989, and a food court was added in 1990. Sears, Maison Blanche, Jordan Marsh, and Burdine's department stores anchor the two-level mall with its 165 specialty shops. *451 Altamonte Ave., Altamonte Springs (½ mi east of I–4 on Rte. 436), tel. 407/830–4400.*

Altamonte Mall, **2**
Belz Factory Outlet, **6**
Church Street
Exchange, **4**
Crossroads, **13**
Dansk, **9**
Denim World, **8**
Disney Village
Marketplace, **14**
Edwin Watts Golf, **10**
Flea World, **1**
The Florida Mall, **7**
Mercado
Mediterranean
Village, **12**
Marketplace, **11**
Old Town, **15**
Park Avenue, **3**
Quality Outlet, **5**

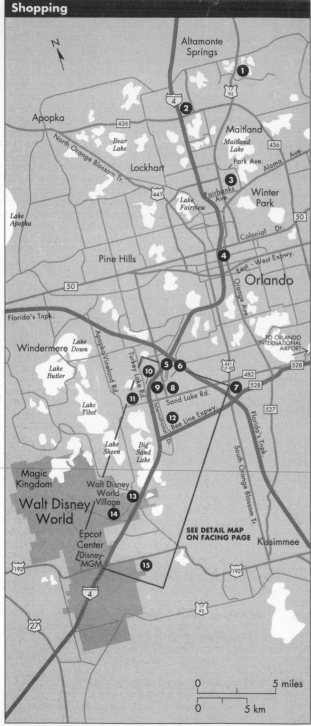

Shopping (detail)

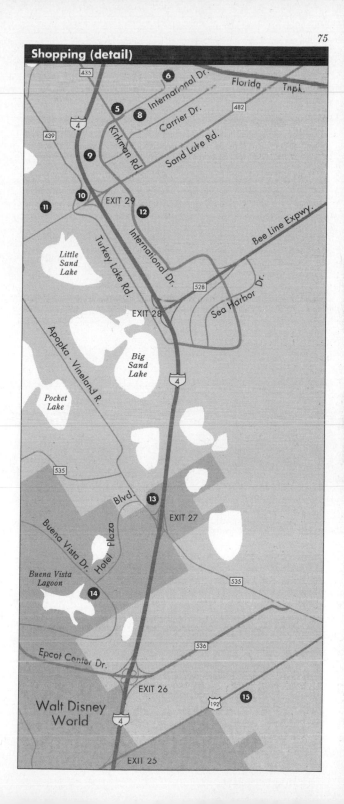

Shopping Villages

These are quaint, themed shopping centers filled with gift shops, clothing stores, and restaurants. They are primarily for tourists, with tourist prices, but they are much more pleasant and relaxed than the malls.

Disney Village Marketplace. If you are looking for one-stop Disney shopping, this is the place. **Mickey's Character Shop** is the largest Disney merchandise store in the world. Seventeen shops selling art, fashions, and crafts are nestled in an attractive setting on Buena Vista Lagoon. Artisans such as the crystal cutters in **Cristal Arts** demonstrate their skills throughout the day. The prices are no better or worse than they are anywhere in the country. While parents shop, kids can rent watercraft at the marina. It is relatively quiet during the early part of the day, but it gets busier as the day goes on, especially with adjoining Pleasure Island, with its clubs, eateries, theaters, and shops. *Lake Buena Vista, tel. 407/828–3058. Open daily 9:30 AM–10 PM.*

Church Street Exchange. This is a decorative, brassy, Victorian-themed "festival marketplace" filled with more than 50 specialty shops. At **The Pearl Factory** you can choose a pearl from an oyster to create your own pearl ring, pendant, or earrings. The factory also offers an informative explanation of how oysters make pearls. **Candlelite** demonstrates how its refillable, hand-carved, and unique candles are designed. Perhaps the best demonstration is at **The Fudgery,** where free samples are distributed during a light-hearted look at the process of making fudge. **Units** is a popular store with a variety of colors and accessories to mix and match outfits on a one-size-fits-all basis. Handcrafted pewter originals by Michael Ricker are on sale at **Pewter by Ricker.** *Church St. Station, 129 W. Church St., tel. 407/422–2434. Open 11 –11.*

Mercado Mediterranean Village. Spanish-style architecture houses more than 50 specialty shops featuring all sorts of gifts from Chinese pottery to broadswords from Toledo (Spain, that is). Six restaurants and a dinner theater are found along the walkway that circles the festival courtyard, where live entertainment can be enjoyed at different times throughout the day. Full-service restaurants include **Royal Orleans,** which serves Cajun fare, and **Bergamo's Italian Restaurant,** serving Continental cuisine. The food court is clean, quick, and large, and it offers a diverse selection of food from around the world. *Mercado Mediterranean Village, 8445 International Dr., tel. 407/345–9337. Open daily 10–10.*

The Marketplace. This outdoor shopping center is super-convenient for taking care of all your basic necessities in one spot near International Drive. Stores include a pharmacy, post office, one-hour film processor, stationery and card store, bakery, and 24-hour supermarket. Also in the Marketplace are two good restaurants: **Christini's** (tel. 407/345–8770) and **Darbar** (tel. 407/345–8128). *7600 Dr. Phillips Blvd., Orlando. Take I–4 or International Dr. to Sand Lake Rd. It is two stoplights west of the I–4 Sand Lake exit.*

The Crossroads of Lake Buena Vista. Located across the street from the entrance to the hotels at Lake Buena Vista, these 11 restaurants and 13 shops are convenient for tourists. The upscale and casual shops are geared toward sun and surf, electronics, and children. But the necessities, such as a 24-hour grocery and pharmacy, post office, bank, and cleaners, are also there, saving long trips to town. *Exit 27 on I–4 at S.R. 535.*

Old Town. A well-designed, turn-of-the-century, old-Florida-theme complex with brick streets and historical architecture, this is a good bet for visitors to the Kissimmee area. There are more than 60 specialty shops, an Elvis Presley museum, a train museum, an antique carousel, an ice cream parlor, candy store, and a 1950s nostalgia nightclub, **Little Darlin's.** *5770 Irlo Bronson Memorial Hwy., Kissimmee (east of I–4), tel. 407/396-4888; 800/843-4202; or in FL, 800/331-5093. Open daily 10 AM–10 PM.*

Park Avenue. Although longtime residents complain that the avenue is beginning to resemble a mall as the local one-of-a-kind stores are replaced by upscale chains, this posh shopping district is still delightful. Stroll past such stores as Banana Republic, Benetton, The Gap, Orvis, Laura Ashley, and Ralph Lauren, then step into the little courtyards to find restaurants, bookshops, galleries, and little shops like **Vieille Provence** (121 E. Welbourne Ave., tel. 407/628-3858), a French country store, or **BeBe's** (311 Park Ave. S, tel. 407/628-1680), for unusual items for children.

6 Sports and Fitness

Participant Sports

Golf and Tennis Many resort hotels let nonguests use their golf and tennis facilities. Some hotels are affiliated with a particular country club, offering preferred rates. If you are staying near a resort with facilities you want to use, call and inquire about their policies. Be sure always to call in advance to reserve courts and tee times. What follows is a list of the best places open to the public.

Golf **Golfpac** (Box 940490, Maitland 32794, tel. 407/660–8559) packages golf vacations and prearranges tee-times at more than 30 courses around Orlando.

Walt Disney World's three championship courses—all on the PGA Tour route—are among the busiest and most expensive in the region. Greens fees are $70, $32 after 3 PM.

Golf lessons are given in small groups at the two Disney Inn courses, the Magnolia and the Palm. Private lessons are available both at these courses and at the Lake Buena Vista Club. There is also a nine-hole executive course on artificial turf with natural turf greens for $13. For private lessons at the Lake Buena Vista Club, phone 407/828–3741. For all other information, phone 407/824–2270.

Two more 18-hole, par 72 courses, designed by noted golf architects Pete Dye and Tom Fazio, are scheduled to open beginning this year.

Poinciana Golf & Racquet Resort (500 Cypress Pkwy., tel. 407/933–5300) has a par-72 course about 18 miles southeast of Disney World.

Grenelefe Golf and Tennis Resort (3200 S.R. 546, Haines City, tel. 813/422–7511; 800/237–9549; in FL, 800/282–7875), located about 45 minutes from Orlando, has three 18-hole courses over gentle hills. Make the West Course (18 holes, par 72, 7,325 yards) your first choice. East Course is 6,802 yards, par 72, and the South Course is 6,869 yards, par 71.

Orange Lake Country Club (8505 W. U.S. 192, Kissimmee, tel. 407/239–0000) offers three nine-hole courses and is about five minutes from Walt Disney World's main entrance. The Orange (with a 118-yard island hole) and the Cypress is the most challenging 18-hole combination. All three courses are par 36 and about 3,300 yards.

Other challenging courses open to the public are **Marriott's Orlando World Center** (1 World Center Dr., Orlando, tel. 407/239–4200; 800/228–9290), 6,265-yards; **Cypress Creek Country Club** (5353 Vineland Rd., tel. 407/425–2319), 6,952 yards; **Hunter's Creek Golf Course** (14401 Sports Club Way, tel. 407/240–4653), 7,432 yards; **Timacuan Golf and Country Club** (550 Timacuan Blvd., Lake Mary, tel. 407/321–0010), 7,027 yards; **Wedgefield Golf and Country Club** (20550 Maxim Pkwy., tel. 407/568–2116), 6,378 yards; **MetroWest Country Club** (2100 S. Hiawassee Rd., tel. 407/297–0052), 7,051 yards.

Tennis **Disney Inn** (tel. 407/824–1469) has two courts; **Village Clubhouse** (tel. 407/828–3741) has three; the **Dolphin** and **Swan** (tel. 407/934–6000) share eight; the **Grand Floridian** (tel. 407/824–2438) has two composition courts; the **Yacht and Beach Club** (tel. 407/934–8000) has two; **Fort Wilderness Campground** (tel.

407/824–2900) has two (first come, first served); and the **Contemporary Resort** (tel. 407/824–3578) has six, where private and group lessons are available. All the courts have lights and are open until 10 PM. Racquets can be rented by the hour.

Orange Lake Country Club (8505 W. U.S. 192, Kissimmee, tel. 407/239–2255) has 16 all-weather courts, 10 of them lighted.

Marsha Park Tennis Center at Lake Cane (Conroy and Turkey Lake Rds., tel. 407/351–4303) has seven hard courts.

Orlando Tennis Center (649 W. Livingston St., tel. 407/246–2162) has 16 lighted courts (9 clay, $2.62 for 90 minutes; 7 hard, $1.56 for 90 minutes); 2 racquetball courts, and 4 tennis pros. Lessons: $56 an hour, $28 for 30 minutes. Away from the touristy side of town are **Red Bug Park** (3800 Red Bug Lake Rd., Casselberry, tel. 407/695–7113) and **Sanlando Park** (401 W. Highland St., Altamonte Springs, tel. 407/869–5966), both run by Seminole County. Red Bug has 16 lighted hard courts and Sanlando has 24. Each has lighted racquetball courts. Cost for tennis: $2 an hour per court, weekdays 8–5 and all day on weekends; $4 an hour per court weekdays 5–10. Racquetball: $4 an hour per court.

Health Clubs   **Radisson Inn Aquatic Center** (Radisson Inn, 8444 International Dr., tel. 407/345–0417) has Nautilus, free-weights, racquetball, swimming, and tennis. $10 a day for all facilities; $30 a week. Racquetball is $8 an hour extra between 4:30 and 8 PM, and $5 after 8 PM.

Walt Disney World's Olympiad Health Club (tel. 407/824–3410) at the Contemporary has Nautilus and whirlpool and is open Mon.–Sat. 9–6. Facilities cost $5, with an additional $5 for use of the whirlpools. The **Magic Mirror** at the Disney Inn has free weights and cardiovascular equipment. Hours are daily 8:30–6, at $4 per day or $10 for the length of your stay. The **St. John's Health Spa** at the Grand Floridian is $5 per visit or $10 for length of stay, but open only to guests of the hotel. The **Village Clubhouse** has Universal equipment and is open daily 7–6. The **Ship Shape** in the Yacht and Beach Club has exercise machines, sauna, spa, steam room, and aerobics classes. Hours are daily 6:30 AM–9:30 PM, at $5 a day or $10 for length of your stay. The Dolphin offers **Body by Jake,** which includes aerobics, weights, and personal trainers from 8 AM to 10 PM, and the Swan also has aerobics classes and exercise equipment.

Water Sports   Marinas at **Caribbean Beach Resort, Contemporary Resort, Fort Wilderness, Polynesian Village, Grand Floridian, Yacht and Beach Club,** and **Walt Disney World Shopping Village** rent sunfish, catamarans, motor-powered pontoon boats, pedal boats, and tiny two-passenger Water Sprites—a hit with kids—for use on Bay Lake, the adjoining Seven Seas Lagoon, Club Lake, Lake Buena Vista, or Buena Vista Lagoon. The Polynesian Village marina rents outrigger canoes. Fort Wilderness rents canoes at $4 an hour and $9 per day for paddling along the placid canals in the area. For water-skiing reservations ($65 per hour), phone 407/824–1000.

Airboat Rentals (4266 Vine St., Kissimmee, tel. 407/847–3672) rents airboats ($20 an hour) and canoes for use on the Shingle Creek, with views of giant cypress trees and Spanish moss.

Ski Holidays (13323 Lake Bryan Dr., tel. 407/239–4444) has water skiing, jet-skiing, and parasailing on a private lake next to

Disney World; boat rental, $60 per hour. Also available are wave runners, jet boats, and Jet-skis. To get there, take I–4 to the Lake Buena Vista exit, turn south on Route 535 toward Kissimmee. Turn left onto a private dirt road about 300 yards down on the left.

Splash 'N' Ski (10000 Turkey Lake Rd., tel. 407/352–1494) rents Jet-skis ($40 per 30 minutes), sailboards ($25 for a half day), and boats (waterskiing, $45 per 30 minutes); and has a ski ramp and slalom course on Sand Lake. Get off I–4 at Exit 29 and take Sand Lake Road west. Turn left at Turkey Lake Road. It is next to Sonesta Village Hotel.

Rent a powerful seven-seater ski boat at **Sanford Boat Rentals** (4370 Carraway Pl., Sanford, tel. 407/321–5906, in FL 800/237–5105) and travel up the St. Johns River. Houseboats and pontoons are available for day, overnight, weekend, or week-long trips. Pontoon and ski boats $60 for 4 hours or $100 per day; 44-foot houseboat $350 per day, $560 for 2 days, $1,000 weekly. Rates vary seasonally.

Go Vacations (2280 Hontoon Dr., DeLand, tel. 904/730–9422 or 800/262–3454) rents luxury houseboats on the St. Johns River. Among the packages is a $795 weekend deal and a weekly price of $1,295. Rates vary seasonally.

Hontoon Landing Marina (2317 River Ridge Rd., DeLand, tel. 800/458–2474; in FL, 800/248–2474) also rents luxury houseboats to cruise the St. Johns River with rates ranging from $400 daily to $1,395 weekly. Prices go down December–February. Get off I–4 at Exit 56 and go west on Highway 44 through DeLand. Turn left on Hontoon Road, then turn left on River Ridge Road and go to the end.

Near Kissimmee, you can rent an airboat ($20 per hour) and explore the backwaters of Osceola County at **U-Drive** (tel. 407/847–3672), six miles east of I–4 on U.S. 192. There are also canoes ($5 an hour) and small electric boats ($16 per hour).

Fishing   **Fort Wilderness Campground** (tel. 407/824–2900) is the starting point for two-hour fishing trips, departing at 8 AM and 3 PM. Boat, equipment, and guide for up to five anglers costs $110.

Central Florida is covered with freshwater lakes and rivers teeming with all kinds of fish, from largemouth black bass to perch, catfish, sunfish, and pike. Lake Tohopekaliga is a popular camping and fishing destination and convenient for most visitors to Central Florida. Don't bother trying to pronounce it, it is Lake Toho to the locals. Among the best fishing camps are **Red's Fish Camp** (4715 Kissimmee Park Rd., St. Cloud, tel. 407/892–8795); **Richardson's Fish Camp** (1550 Scotty's Rd., Kissimmee, tel. 407/846–6540); **Scotty's Fish Camp & Mobil Home Park** (1554 Scotty's Rd., Kissimmee, tel. 407/847–3840); and **East Lake Fish Camp** (3705 Big Bass Rd., Kissimmee, tel. 407/348–2040).

Bass Challenger Guide (Box 679155, Orlando, tel. 407/273–8045) takes you out in boats equipped with drinks and tackle. Transportation can be arranged to and from their location. Half-day (one or two persons) from $125, full day from $175. Their guarantee is "No bass, no pay!"

Bass Bustin' Guide (5935 Swoffield Dr., Orlando, tel. 407/281–0845) provides boat, tackle, transportation, and amenities for bass fishing on local lakes. And they guarantee fish! Half day from $125, full day from $175.

Bicycling The most scenic bike riding in Orlando is on Disney World property, along roads that take you past forests, lakes, golf courses, and Disney's wooded resort villas and campgrounds. Bikes are available for rent at **Caribbean Beach Resort** (tel. 407/934–3400), **Fort Wilderness Bike Barn** (tel. 407/824–2742), and **Walt Disney World Village Villa Center** (tel. 407/824–6947). Bike rental $3 an hour, $7 per day.

Jogging Walt Disney World has several scenic jogging trails. Pick up jogging maps at any Disney resort. **Fort Wilderness** (tel. 407/824–2900) has a 2.3-mile jogging course with plenty of fresh air and woods as well as numerous exercise stations along the way.

Horseback Riding Grand Cypress Equestrian Center (tel. 407/239–4608) offers hunter, jumper, and dressage private lessons ($30 for 30 minutes, $50 for an hour). Novice ($25 an hour) and advanced ($30 an hour) trails are available.

Fort Wilderness Campground Resort (tel. 407/824–2803) in Disney World offers tame trail rides through backwoods and along lakesides. Open to the general public. Call in advance to arrange an outing. Rides at 9, 10:30, noon, 1, and 2. Cost is $13 per person for 45 minutes. Children must be over nine.

Poinciana Horse World (3705 Poinciana Blvd., Kissimmee, tel. 407/847–4343) takes visitors for hour rides along old logging trails near Kissimmee. Cost is $14.

Ice Skating **Orlando Ice Skating Palace** (3123 W. Colonial Dr., Parkwood Shopping Plaza, Orlando, tel. 407/299–5440) isn't the most attractive rink, but if you are homesick for a winter chill, this should do the trick. *Admission: weekdays $4.95 adults, $4.45 children, Fri.–Sat. $5.95 adults, $5.45 children; $1.50 skate rentals. Open Wed.–Fri. 7:30–10:30 PM; Sat. 12:30–3:30, 4–7, and 11 PM–1 AM; Sun. 2–5.*

Ice Rink International (Dowdy Pavilion, 7503 Canada Ave., Orlando, tel. 407/363–7465 or 407/352–9393). Public sessions Wednesday–Sunday. Call for times and prices.

Spectator Sports

Jai Alai **Orlando–Seminole Jai–Alai.** The sport is fun to watch even if you don't bet. *Admission: $1 general, $2 reserved seating. Open May–Jan. at 7:20 nightly except Sun., with noon matinees Mon., Thurs., and weekends Fern Park, off I–4 about 20 minutes north of Orlando, tel. 407/331–9191.*

Dog Racing **Sanford Orlando Kennel Club** (301 Dog Track Rd., Longwood, tel. 407/831–1600) has dog racing and betting nightly at 7:30 PM except Sunday. *Admission $1. Open Dec.–May; matinees Mon., Wed., and Sat. at 1 PM.*

Seminole Greyhound Park (2000 Seminola Blvd., Casselberry, tel. 407/699–4510) is a newer track with racing nightly at 7:45 except Sunday. *Admission $1 general, $2 clubhouse, children half price. Open May–Oct. Weekday matinees have been changing times each year; most recently they have been Mon., Wed., and Sat. at 1 PM.*

Basketball **Orlando Magic** (Box 76, Orlando, FL 32802, tel. 407/839–3900) joined the National Basketball Association in the 1989–90 season. The team plays in the new 15,077-seat Orlando Arena. *Admission $8–$28. Exit I–4 at Amelia; the arena is two blocks west of the interstate.*

Baseball The **Orlando SunRays** are Minnesota's Class AA Southern League affiliate. They play baseball at Tinker Field. *Exit I–4 at Colonial Ave. (Hwy. 50), go west to Tampa Ave. and south on Tampa to the stadium. Tel. 407/849–6346.*

The **Osceola Astros** are Houston's Class A team in the Florida State League. They play at Osceola County Stadium in Kissimmee. *Tel. 407/933–5500.*

The **Baseball City Royals** are Kansas City's Class A team in the Florida State League. *Just 30 min from Disney World, at the intersection of I–4 and U.S. 27, tel. 407/648–5151 or 813/424–2424.*

Football **Orlando Thunder** play in the World League of American Football. Games are held from March to June at Orlando stadium. *Tel. 407/841–2078.*

7 Dining

Many of Orlando's finest restaurants are located in the stylish hotels in the heavily touristed areas. These dining establishments like to flaunt their sophisticated menus and wine lists, and show off their big-city tastes. The thing is, many of them actually are as good as one can expect from the best chain hotel restaurants anywhere in the United States. If you want convenience, decent food, and a cosmopolitan atmosphere, hotel restaurants are a safe bet. If, however, you're watching your pennies or enjoy an atmosphere with a certain regional flavor, try some local spots in Orlando. You may have to drive to find a restaurant with much character, but you'll be rewarded with a taste of Orlando, and considerable savings.

The dress code is indicated after each restaurant's address below. Ties are always optional, though men on the far side of 30 commonly wear them. "Casual," which applies to all but the fanciest places in Orlando, means comfortably presentable—avoiding shorts, sneakers, and T-shirts. "Informal" means wear whatever you please.

It is always a good idea to make reservations, even on a slow night; otherwise a large group may arrive moments before you, and keep you waiting on line. Orlando is not a big town, but getting to places is almost always complicated, so always call for directions. The budget-conscious should consider dining before 6 PM, when many area restaurants offer early-bird specials.

If you want to try some local specialties, consider stone crabs, pompano (a mild white fish), Apalachicola oysters, small tasty Florida lobsters, and conch chowder. Fresh hearts of palm are a treat, too.

The most highly recommended restaurants are indicated by a star ★.

Category	Cost*
Very Expensive	over $40
Expensive	$30–$40
Moderate	$20–$30
Inexpensive	under $20

*per person, excluding drinks, service, and 6% sales tax

The Walt Disney World Area

These are restaurants close to Disney World, situated along International Drive or near Kissimmee, Disney Maingate, and Lake Buena Vista.

American **Empress Lilly.** Disney's 220-foot, 19th-century Mississippi-style riverboat is a popular tourist dining spot permanently moored at the far end of Walt Disney World Shopping Village, right on Buena Vista Lagoon. Though its bright red paddle wheel has never moved the boat an inch, much attention was paid to make it look like an elegant, old-fashioned Victorian showboat, complete with brass lamps, burgundy velvet loveseats, and mahogany wood. The boat has several restau-

Arthur's 27, **17**
Beeline Diner, **25**
Border Cantina, **2**
Cattle Ranch, **7**
Chalet Suzanne, **22**
Chatham's Place, **12**
Christini's, **14**
Darbar, **15**
Dux, **26**
Empress Lilly, **20**
Gary's Duck Inn, **9**
Hard Rock Cafe
Orlando, **10**
Hemingway's, **18**
Jordan's Grove, **5**
La Coquina, **19**
Le Coq Au Vin, **8**
Ming Court, **24**
Murphy Jim's, **1**
Palm Terrace, **21**
Park Plaza Gardens, **3**
Phoenician, **13**
Pizzeria Uno, **6**
Ran-Getsu, **27**
Rolandos, **4**
Rossi's, **11**
Siam Orchid, **28**
Sweet Basil, **23**
Victoria and
Albert's, **16**

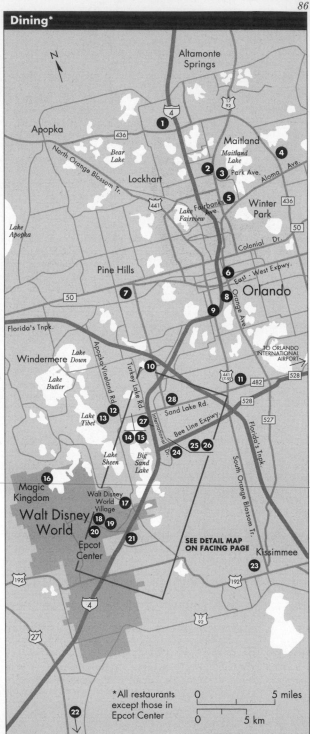

Dining*

*All restaurants
except those in
Epcot Center

Dining (detail) *

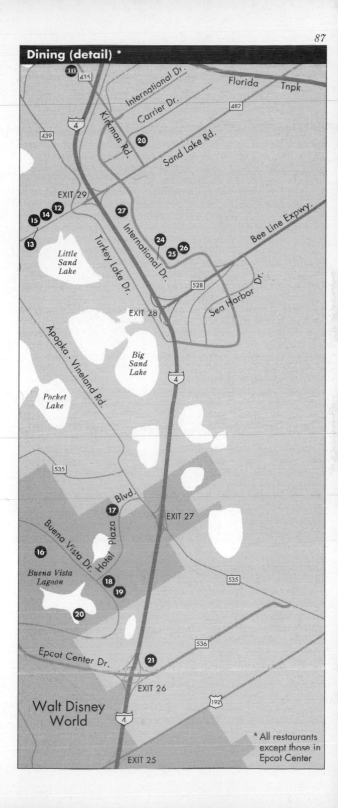

rants and lounges. Beef is served in Steerman's Quarters, and seafood in Fisherman's Deck. Only 5% of the tables are open for reservations, two days in advance. Visitors without reservations should arrive early, add their names to the list, and go and listen to banjo music in Baton Rouge Lounge. The food is predictable, but dining here can be a fun, enjoyable experience for large families or groups that want a decent meal but do not want to feel inhibited by a stuffy atmosphere. The third restaurant on the showboat is the Empress Room, a plush, Louis XV-style dining room filled with gilded reminders of another age. It is a small, luxurious (if gaudy) setting that might bring out the Rhett Butler or Scarlett O'Hara in you, but you will wish that the food measured up to the prices. The menu reads elegantly, featuring such specialties as duck, pheasant, venison, and various seafood dishes—but the food is unlikely to live up to expectations suggested by the elegance of the setting. *Walt Disney World Shopping Village, tel. 407/828–3900. Steerman's Quarters and Fisherman's Deck: Dress: casual. Only a few reservations accepted. AE, MC, V. Moderate. Empress Room: Jacket required. Reservations required, up to a month in advance. AE, DC, MC, V. Expensive.*

Continental **Arthur's 27.** Situated on the top floor of the Buena Vista Palace Hotel, Arthur's 27 offers visitors not only an elegant meal but also one of the best views of the Magic Kingdom and Epcot. The fixed-price, four-course Continental dinner is $45, and the six-course Continental dinner is $60, *without* drinks; if you order à la carte, expect to pay more. Service and quality are first class, though bordering on the pretentious. The wine list is formidable, featuring everything from reasonable California wines to some vintage Bordeaux that could be sold at auction. Specialties include venison and sautéed breast of duck with honey-ginger sauce. Arthur's is very popular on weekends, and there is only one seating per night, so reservations are at a premium and should be made at the same time that you reserve your room. Dinners last several hours, so make sure you're with someone you like. *Buena Vista Palace Hotel, Walt Disney World Village, tel. 407/827–3450. Jacket required. Reservations strongly advised. AE, DC, MC, V. Very Expensive.*

Victoria and Albert's. The surroundings and treatment are more impressive than the food. The prix fixe menu changes daily but always offers a choice of beef, seafood, or poultry. The prices tend to be high, but they help pay for the Royal Doulton china, Sambonet silver, Schott-Zweisel crystal, and turn-of-the-century costumes for your servers—a maid and butler named Victoria and Albert. Beware of the ceiling's dome effect—it allows others in the small restaurant to hear every word you say. *Grand Floridian Beach Resort, Walt Disney World, tel. 407/824–2823. Jacket required. Reservations required. AE, MC, V. Very Expensive.*

La Coquina. This is a hotel restaurant with an emphasis on seafood and serious sauces. One popular meat specialty is loin of lamb with eggplant and goat cheese in grape leaves, served with grilled *polenta* (Italian-style cooked cornmeal). Best bet here is Sunday brunch—a cornucopia of fruits, vegetables, pastries, pâtés, smoked fish, and a number of dishes cooked before your eyes. The $29 brunch is served with Domaine Chandon champagne; the $85 brunch with all the Dom Perignon champagne you can consume. If you're hungry and thirsty enough, you just might be able to put them out of business. Hyatt Regency Grand Cypress Resort, *1 Grand Cypress Blvd., Orlando, tel. 407/239-1234. Jacket required. Reservations advised. AE, DC, MC, V. Expensive.*

Kosher **Palm Terrace.** This is a Kosher restaurant supervised by a rabbi of the Orthodox Union. Diners who are not guests at the Hyatt Orlando pay a fixed price of $38 (half-price half portions for children 3–12) for Shabbas meals. Meals must be prepaid on Fridays and reservations are required a half hour before candle-lighting. Kosher breakfast and lunch items are available next door at the **Marketplace Deli** from 6 AM to 1 AM. (The Hyatt also offers a schul, with services held twice daily.) *Hyatt Orlando, 6375 Irlo Bronson Memorial Hwy., Kissimmee, tel. 407/396-1234. Dress: casual. Reservations required. AE, DC, MC, V. Moderate.*

Seafood **Hemingway's.** Located by the pool at the Hyatt Regency Grand Cypress, this restaurant serves up all sorts of sea creatures from conch, scallops, and squid to grouper, pompano, and monkfish. In addition to the regular menu, Hemingway's also has what is called a "Cuisine Naturelle" menu, featuring dishes that are low in fat, calories, sodium, and cholesterol—recipes that are approved by the American Heart Association and Weight Watchers. What more could you want, other than a big hot-fudge sundae for dessert? *Hyatt Regency Grand Cypress Resort, 1 Grand Cypress Blvd., Orlando, tel. 407/239-1234. Dress: casual. Reservations advised. AE, DC, MC, V. Moderate–Expensive.*

Epcot Center

World Showcase offers some of the finest dining to be found not only in Walt Disney World but in the entire Orlando area. The problem is that the restaurants are often very crowded and difficult to book. Many of them are operated by the same people who own internationally famous restaurants in their home countries. The top-of-the-line places, such as those in the French, Italian, and Japanese pavilions, can be expensive, but they are not as pricey as comparable restaurants in large, cosmopolitan cities such as Paris or New York. One good thing about Epcot's restaurants, besides the food, is that most of them have limited-selection children's menus with dramatically lower prices, so bringing the kids along to dinner won't break the bank.

Visitors are not expected to go all the way back to their hotels to change and clean up and then return for dinner, so casual dress is not only permitted but expected in all of the restaurants, even the finest.

If you want to eat in one of the more popular restaurants, it will be much easier to get a reservation for lunch than for dinner. It won't be quite the same experience, but it will be cheaper. Another way to get a table is to have lunch before noon, and dinner before 6 PM or after 8 PM.

Both lunch and dinner reservations are strongly recommended at any of the finer restaurants in Epcot, and even at some of the not-so-fine. Making them, particularly in a busy season, can be time consuming. Reservations are accepted on a first-come, first-served basis for both lunch and dinner. Unless you are staying at one of the Disney World hotels, you cannot reserve in advance of the day on which you wish to eat, and you can't book by phone. Instead, you must head for Earth Station at the base of Spaceship Earth as soon as you get to Epcot. In Earth Station you will find a bank of computer screens called WorldKey Information. This is where things can get ugly. You need to stand in line to get to one of these screens and place the reservation, and the lines form very early. On busy days, most of the top restaurants are filled within an hour of Epcot's official opening time, so if you want to be sure of getting a reservation, you may have to line up well ahead of Epcot's actual opening time (which, as you may remember, may be as much as an hour ahead of the *published* opening time). Then, once you're through the gate, make a mad dash for the WorldKey computer terminals. If there is a long line when you get to Earth Station, remember that on the far side of Future World, just before the bridge to World Showcase, is an outdoor kiosk with five WorldKey terminals that few people notice. There is also another WorldKey kiosk on the far side of the Port of Entry gift shop, near the boat dock for the water taxi to Morocco. Having made the reservations, you can wipe the beads of sweat from your brow and begin to enjoy your day at Epcot.

It is also possible to reserve in person at a restaurant on the day you want to dine. The problem is that most restaurants don't open until 10 or 11 AM, and by then, in a busy season, all tables will be gone. Of course, it's always worth stopping by during the day and hoping someone has just cancelled.

If you are a guest at a Disney-owned hotel or at one of the Walt Disney World Hotel Plaza hotels, you can avoid the battle of the WorldKey by booking a table by phone (tel. 407/828–4000). Remember that if you are staying at one of these resorts you cannot make a same-day reservation by phone, but must book either one or two days in advance between noon and 9 PM. When making reservations, you'll be asked your name, resort, and room number. The restaurant will ask to see your resort identification card, so don't do something silly like leave it in your hotel room.

No matter how you book, try to show up at the restaurant a bit early to be sure of getting your table. You can pay with American Express, MasterCard, Visa, and, of course, cash. If you're a guest of an on-site hotel—both those owned by Disney and those that are not—you can charge the tab to your room.

British **Rose and Crown.** This is a very popular, friendly, British pub where visitors and Disney employees come at the end of the day to knock off a pint of crisp Bass Ale or blood-thickening Guinness Stout with a few morsels of Stilton cheese. "Wenches" serve up simple pub fare, such as steak-and-kidney pie, beef tenderloin, and fish and chips. The Rose and Crown sits on the shore of the lagoon, so on warm days it's nice to lunch on the patio at the water's edge and enjoy the soft breeze. Dark wood floors, pub chairs, and brass lamps create the warmest, most homey atmosphere in Epcot. The place is so friendly and comfortable that people come just to relax at the bar and chat with anyone who is around. The food is relatively inexpensive, especially at lunch, and the terrace has a great view of Illumi-Nations, so all things considered, it's one of the best finds in Epcot. Lunch and dinner entrees range between $10.75 and $18.50. *Moderate.*

French **Bistro de Paris.** Located on the second floor of the French pavilion, above Chefs de France (*see* below), this is a relatively quiet and charming spot for lunch or dinner. The Bistro specializes in regional cooking from southern France. A favorite is steamed filet of fresh grouper with tomato, mushrooms, fresh herbs, and white wine sauce, served with a rice pilaf. The wines are moderately priced and available by the glass. Lunch entrees $12.25–$20.25, dinner entrees $18.25–$24.50. *Expensive.*

Chefs de France. Three of France's most famous culinary artists came together to create this French restaurant. The most renowned of the three, Paul Bocuse, operates one restaurant north of Lyon and two in Tokyo, and has published several famous books on French cuisine. Another, Gaston Lenôtre, has gained eminence for his pastries and ice creams. The third of this culinary triumvirate, Roger Vergée, operates one of France's most highly touted restaurants, near Cannes. The three don't actually prepare each meal, but they were the ones who created the menu and carefully trained the chefs, and they look in frequently to make sure it's all up to snuff. Some of the most popular classic dishes are roast duck with prunes and wine sauce; beef filet with fresh ground pepper, raisins, and Armagnac sauce; and filet of grouper topped with salmon-vegetable mousse and baked in puff pastry. Lunch entrees $6.50–$12.25, dinner entrees $13.95–$19.55. *Expensive.*

German **Biergarten.** This popular spot boasts Oktoberfest 365 days a year. Visitors sit at long communal tables and are served by waitresses in typical Bavarian garb. The cheerful—some would say raucous—atmosphere is what one would expect from a place where performers yodel, sing, and dance to the rhythms of an oompah band. The crowd, pounding pitchers of beer or wine while consuming hot pretzels and hearty German fare, is usually pretty active when audience participation is called for, and just as active when it is not. Lunch and dinner entrees range between $12.95 and $17.95. *Moderate.*

Italian **L'Originale Alfredo di Roma Ristorante.** This is a World Show-
★ case hot spot with the most dynamic atmosphere and some of the finest food in Disney World. During dinner waiters skip around singing Italian songs and bellowing arias. At lunch you don't get the musical show, but the Italian waiters are usually entertaining enough to be a side show by themselves. If you are a pasta fan, this is the place for you. The restaurant is named for the same man who invented the now-classic fettuccine Alfredo, a pasta served with a sauce of cream, butter, and loads of freshly grated Parmesan cheese. It was this outstanding dish that made Alfredo de Lelio famous when he opened his original L'Originale Alfredo di Roma in 1914. Today it is operated by his grandson. Other than pasta, you should try *lo chef consiglia* (the Chef's Selection), which consists of an appetizer of spaghetti or fettuccine, a mixed green salad, and a chicken or veal entree. The most popular veal dish is *piccata di vitello*—veal thinly sliced and pan-fried with lemon and white wine. Lunch entrees $6.75–$16.95, dinner entrees $11.50–$20.50. *Expensive.*

Japanese **Mitsukoshi.** This isn't just a restaurant, it's a complex of dining
★ areas on the second floor above the Mitsukoski Department Store. Each of the five dining rooms (on your left as you enter) has four tables that seat eight and are equipped with a grill on which chefs prepare meats and fish with acrobatic precision.

It's an American's idea of the real Japan, but fun nonetheless, especially if you are with a large group. Smaller parties may prefer going to the Tempura Kiku dining room on the right and sampling the tempura shrimp or thinly sliced Kabuki beef while sipping hot sake and enjoying a great view of the lagoon and Spaceship Earth. Lunch entrees $6.75–$12, dinner entrees $12.50–$26. *Moderate.*

Mexican **San Angel Inn.** The lush, tropical surrounding—cool, dark, almost surreal—makes this perhaps the most exotic restaurant in Disney World. The ambience is at once romantic and lively. Tables are candlelit, but close together, and the restaurant is open to the "sky" in the inside of the pavilion, where folk singers perform and musicians play guitars or xylophones. The best seats are along the outer edge of the restaurant, opposite the entrance, directly above the "river," with its boats streaming by, and below the Aztec pyramid, with its soft, fiery light evoking a sense of the distant past. The air-conditioning is often on high, so you may want to bring a light sweater. One of the specialties is *Langosta Baja California*—Baja lobster meat sauteed with tomatoes, onions, olives, Mexican peppers, and white wine, and baked in its shell—not exactly the sort of dish that comes to mind when you think of Mexican food. Try the margaritas, and, for dessert, don't miss the chocolate Kahlua mousse pie. Lunch entrees $5.25–$12.50, dinner entrees $10.50–$20.95. *Moderate.*

Moroccan **Marrakesh.** Belly dancers and a three-piece Moroccan band set the mood in this exotic restaurant, where you may feel as though you have stumbled onto the set of *Casablanca*, or the African continent itself. The food is mildly spicy and relatively inexpensive. Try the national dish of Morocco, *couscous*, served with garden vegetables; or *bastila*, an appetizer of sweet-and-spicy pork between many layers of thin pastry, with almonds, saffron, and cinnamon. Lunch and dinner entrees range between $7.50 and $16.95. *Moderate.*

Norwegian **Restaurant Akershus.** Norway's tradition of seafood and cold-meat dishes is highlighted at the restaurant's *koldtbord*, or Norwegian buffet. Hosts and hostesses explain the dishes to guests and suggest which ones go together. It is traditional to make several trips to the *koldtbord*, so there is no need to shovel everything you see onto your plate at one time. The first trip is for appetizers, usually herring. On your next trip choose cold seafood items—try gravlaks, salmon cured with salt, sugar, and dill. Pick up cold salads and meats on your next trip, and then, on your fourth trip, you fill up with hot dishes, usually a choice of lamb, veal, and venison. Desserts are offered à la carte, including cloudberries, delicate, seasonal fruits that grow on the tundra. There are four dining rooms, seating 220 in an impressive copy of Oslo's famous Akershus Castle. Lunch entrees are under $9 and dinners are priced under $15. *Moderate.*

The Orlando Area

The following restaurants are in or near the city of Orlando and cater mostly to a local clientele.

American **Chatham's Place.** The staff at elegant Chatham's Place has a ★ genuine concern that anyone who enters will have a perfect dining experience. The Chatham brothers' expertise shines with such entrées as black grouper with pecan butter, spaghetti al Grecque, and duck breast grilled to crispy perfection. It's a modest space, and the office building exterior belies what's inside, but this is arguably one of Orlando's best. *7575 Dr. Phillips Blvd., Orlando, tel. 407/345-2992. Dress: casual. Reservations strongly advised. MC, V. Moderate-Expensive.*

★ **Jordan's Grove.** This old house was built in 1912 and now holds one of Orlando's most popular restaurants. The menu changes daily and the prix fixe includes a choice of soup or salad, appetizer, entree with vegetables, and dessert. An à la menu was recently added. The changing menu allows for some creative flexing in the kitchen, and few people leave unsatisfied. Wine, the only alcoholic beverage served, is mostly American from smaller estates. *1300 S. Orlando Ave., (U.S. Highway 17-92), Maitland, tel. 407/628-0020. Dress: casual. Reservations advised. AE, DC, MC, V. Moderate-Expensive.*

Murphy Jim's. A tiny restaurant packed with charm, Murphy Jim's offers a creative menu served by an attentive staff. Highlights include jumbo broiled shrimp topped with a lime butter and tequila sauce, and red snapper doused with pineapple butter. Cloth covered tables are set with matching dinnerware, but not matching the next table. Waiters look after each others' tables, making for pleasant and efficient dining. *249 W. State Road 436, Altamonte Springs, tel. 407/862-1668. Dress: casual. Reservations advised. AE, MC, V. Moderate.*

Hard Rock Cafe Orlando. The popular Los Angeles Brat Pack hangout comes to Orlando with the opening of Universal Studios Florida. You can enter the guitar-shape building from the theme park, or from the street. Besides the rock music and rock memorabilia, Orlando's Hard Rock features a Hollywood room. Food includes hamburgers, barbecue, and sandwiches. *Universal Studios Florida, 5800 Kirkman Rd., Orlando, tel. 407/351-7625. Dress: casual. No reservations. AE, MC, V. Inexpensive.*

Chinese **Ming Court.** This is no takeout Chinese, but it is truly fine dining—Oriental style. Although some names of the dishes will sound familiar, creative flairs make each dish unique to Ming Court. Try the jumbo shrimps in lobster sauce flavored with crushed black beans, or the Hunan Kung Pao Chicken with peanuts, cashews, and walnuts. Prices may seem high, but the elegant surroundings—glass walls allow you to look out on the pond and floating gardens—make the check worthwhile. Another plus is that Ming Court is within walking distance of the Orange County Convention Center. *9188 International Dr., Orlando, 407/351-9988. Dress: casual. Reservations advised. AE, DC, MC, V. Moderate.*

Continental **Dux.** In the Peabody Hotel's gourmet restaurant, some crea-
★ tions are innovative, such as the grilled quail with poached quail eggs, served with wild rice in a carrot terrine nest. Others are a trifle self conscious, like the avocado with sautéed salmon, artichoke chips, and champagne caviar sauce. For an entree, consider the baked Florida lobster with chanterelle mushrooms, spinach, and champagne sauce. The selection of California wines is outstanding. *Peabody Hotel, 9801 International Dr., Orlando, tel. 407/352-4000. Jacket required. Reservations strongly advised. AE, DC, MC, V. Expensive.*

Park Plaza Gardens. A trip to Park Avenue—a mini Rodeo Drive—is a must. Dining at Park Plaza Gardens makes you feel even more a part of the upper crust. The dining room is actually a courtyard with a glass roof (contrary to what most people think, Florida is not a great place to dine alfresco), but it feels like you're dining outdoors. Tuxedoed waiters serve such delights as grouper escovitche and roast rack of lamb. The highclass atmosphere is not pretentious. *319 S. Park Ave., Winter Park, tel. 407/645-2475. Dress: casual. Reservations advised. AE, DC, MC, V. Moderate-Expensive.*

Cuban **Rolandos.** Cuban cuisine is Florida's staple, and Rolandos is
★ one of the best places to try it. Black bean soup, dirty rice, chicken with yellow rice, and mincemeat are just a few of the specialties of this cuisine. The name is not an indication of the quality, it's the owner's second restaurant. *870 Semoran Blvd., Casselberry, tel. 407/767-9677. Dress: casual. No reservations. MC, V. Inexpensive.*

French **Le Coq au Vin.** The atmosphere here is mobile-home-modern,
★ but the traditional French fare is first-class, and you can pride yourself on discovering a place few tourists know about but that is nearly always filled with a friendly Orlando clientele. Owners Louis Perrotte and his wife, Magdalena (the hostess), make a charming couple who give the place its warmth and homey personality. Their specialties are homemade chicken liver pâté, fresh rainbow trout with champagne, and roast Long Island duck with green peppercorn sauce. For dessert, try the crème brûlée. *4800 S. Orange Ave., Orlando, tel. 407/851-6980. Dress: casual. Reservations advised. AE, DC, MC, V. Moderate.*

Indian **Darbar.** This lavishly decorated dining room features northern Indian cuisine. In addition to curries and pilafs, Darbar specializes in tandoori cooking—traditional Indian baking in a clay oven. Meats and vegetables are marinated in special sauces overnight and cooked to perfection. If you're unfamiliar with Indian cuisine, this is a good place to begin. Best bet is the tandoori dinner for two, with different types of lamb and chicken. *7600 Dr. Phillips Blvd., Orlando, tel. 407/345-8128. Dress: casual. Reservations advised on weekends. AE, DC, MC, V. Moderate. To get there, take Sand Lake Blvd. (Exit 29 of I-4) and head west to The Marketplace (just after the second stoplight). The restaurant is in the shopping center.*

Italian **Christini's.** For traditional Italian cuisine, this is Orlando's finest. The restaurant is not about to win any awards for decor, but the food couldn't be more fresh, and the service couldn't be more efficient. This is the kind of upscale Italian restaurant you might find in New York. The restaurant makes its own pastas daily and serves them with herbs, vegetables, and freshly grated Parmesan. Specialties include fresh fish; a fish soup with lobster, shrimp, and clams; and veal chops with fresh sage. *7600 Dr. Phillips Blvd., in The Marketplace, tel. 407/ 345-8770. Jacket required. Reservations advised. AE, DC, MC, V. Expensive.*

Japanese **Ran-Getsu.** The best Japanese food in town is served in this palatial setting. The atmosphere may seem a bit self-conscious— an American's idea of the Orient—but the food is fresh and carefully prepared. Sit at the curved, dragon's-tail-shaped sushi bar for the Matsu platter—an assortment of *nigiri*- and *maki*-style sushis—or, if you are with a group, sit Japanese-style at tables overlooking a carp-filled pond and decorative gardens. Specialties are sukiyaki and shabu-shabu, the thinly sliced beef in a boiling seasoned broth, served with vegetables and prepared at your table. If you feel more adventurous, try the deep-fried alligator tail. *8400 International Dr., Orlando, tel. 407/345-0044. Dress: casual. Reservations advised. AE, DC, MC, V. Moderate.*

Mexican **Border Cantina.** A new addition to Park Avenue, Border Cantina is trendy Tex-Mex. If you can forgive the pink walls and neon lights in this third-floor restaurant, you won't have any complaints with the food. The Border does fajitas better than you'll find in most places, and the salsa is a fresh, chunky mix that will suit all tastes. Ask for something hotter if you prefer. *329 S. Park Ave., Winter Park, tel. 407/740-7227. Dress: casual. Reservations advised for parties of 8 or more. AE, MC, V. Inexpensive–Moderate.*

Middle Eastern **Phoenician.** This is the latest addition to the rich culinary clique at The Marketplace. Humus, baba ghanouj, and lebneh dishes top the menu. The best bet is to order a tableful of appetizers *(meza)* and sample as many as possible. *7600 Dr. Phillips Blvd., Suite 142, Orlando, tel. 407/345-1001. Dress: casual. No reservations. AE, MC, V. Inexpensive.*

Pizza **Pizzeria Uno.** It's a chain, but when the pizza tastes this good, you can't hold that against it. The decor is early Chicago, a tribute to the franchise's birthplace. Try the spinaccoli pizza, which gets its name from the two main ingredients: spinach and broccoli. Conveniently located, Pizzeria Uno is on the second level of the Church Street Market. *5 W. Church St., Orlando, tel. 407/839-1800. Dress: casual. No reservations. AE, MC, V. Inexpensive.*

Rossi's. This is a local pizza joint—a garlic-bread-pepperoni-pizza-and-a-pitcher-of-Bud-or-rootbeer type of spot. The food is not about to win any awards, but Rossi's is a good escape from the tourist/hotel scene, and the price is so right. *5919 S. Orange Blossom Trail, Orlando, tel. 407/855-5755. Dress: casual. AE, MC, V. Inexpensive.*

Seafood **Gary's Duck Inn.** When some businessmen decided back in 1968 that they wanted to open a chain of seafood restaurants, they used Gary's as the role model. They changed little about the interior and the menu, but they chose a different name for their restaurants: Red Lobster. Gary's is still independently owned, but the Red Lobster comparison is inevitable. Stick to seafood here; steak is not a specialty. *3974 S. Orange Blossom Trail, Orlando, tel. 407/843-0270. Dress: casual. Reservations advised. AE, MC, V. Moderate.*

Steak **Cattle Ranch.** If you're hungry and looking for a big, thick, juicy, down-home American steak, then "steer" for the Cattle Ranch. It's cheap, and, if you're insanely hungry, it's free. Just take "The 6-pound Challenge," in which you're allowed 75 minutes to eat an entire six-pound steak dinner, including salad, potato, and bread. If you can do it, you won't have to pay a dime. If you can't, it will cost you just over 30 bucks. There is absolutely nothing fancy about this cowboy cafeteria except the steaks that come off the burning orangewood fire. And you won't see another tourist for miles around. *6129 Old Winter Garden Rd., Orlando (2½ blocks west of Kirkman Rd.), tel. 407/298-7334. Closed Sun. and Mon. Dress: casual. Reservations: don't bother. AE, MC, V. Inexpensive.*

Thai **Siam Orchid.** Another in the trend of elegant Oriental restaurants offering fine dining, Siam Orchid has a gorgeous structure and is a bit off the beaten path of International Drive. Waitresses, who wear costumes from their homeland, serve authentic Thai cuisine. Some standouts are the Siam wings appetizer—a chicken wing stuffed to look like a drumstick—and *pla lad prig*, a whole fish, deep-fried and covered with a sauce of red chili, bell peppers, and garlic. If you like your food spicy, say "Thai hot" and grab a fire extinguisher. Otherwise, a request to make a dish spicy will be answered with a smile and only a mild dish. *7575 Republic Dr., Orlando, tel. 407/351–3935. Dress: casual. Reservations advised. AE, DC, MC, V. Moderate.*

24 Hours **Beeline Diner.** This is a slick 1950s-style diner that's always open. It is in the Peabody Hotel, so it's not exactly cheap, but the salads, sandwiches, and griddle foods are tops. Though very busy at times, it can be fun for breakfast or a late-night snack. And for just a little silver you get to play a lot of old tunes on the jukebox. *Peabody Hotel, 9801 International Dr., Orlando, tel. 407/352–4000. Dress: casual. Reservations not necessary. AE, DC, MC, V. Moderate.*

Off the Beaten Track

Lake Wales

★ **Chalet Suzanne.** If you like to drive or are returning from a day at Cypress Gardens, consider making a dinner reservation at this award-winning family-owned country inn and restaurant. It has been expanded bit by quirky bit since it opened in the 1930s, and today it looks like a small Swiss village—right in the middle of Florida's orange belt. The restaurant itself is filled with a hodgepodge of furniture from all over the world. The place settings, china, glasses, chairs, even the tables are of different sizes, shapes, and origins. Strangely, however, it all works together as the expression of a single sensibility. For an appetizer, try broiled grapefruit. Recommended among the seven entrees are chicken Suzanne, shrimp curry, lobster Newburg, shad roe, and filet mignon. Crepes Suzanne are a good bet for dessert. The seven-course meals begin at $40. The wine list offers many excellent choices at reasonable prices. Guests may step into the cellar and taste some of the wines that are being featured that night. Because of its charm and originality, the Chalet Suzanne has earned praise from restaurant critics—and for good reason. This unlikely back-road country inn should provide one of the most memorable dining experiences one can have in Orlando. *U.S. 27 north of Lake Wales, about 10 mi past Cypress Gardens turnoff, tel. 813/676–6011. Jacket required. Reservations advised. AE, CE, DC, MC, V. Expensive. Closed Mon. during summer.*

Kissimmee

★ **Sweet Basil.** Standing apart from the other fast-food restaurants, Sweet Basil has creative cuisine that's designed to take little time. Red snapper Provençale and chicken diavolo are standouts. A specialty of the house is the painted dessert. Cheesecakes and pies are served on a vanilla sauce painted with chocolate-sauce-and-raspberry-coulis drawings of cherry blossoms. *1009 W. Vine St., Kissimmee, tel. 407/846–1116. Dress: casual. Reservations advised. AE, MC, V. Moderate.*

8 Lodging

Introduction

To stay within Disney World or without—that is the question.

The law of inertia seems to keep most Disney World guests within its realm. And if you are coming to Orlando for only a few days and are interested solely in the Magic Kingdom, Epcot, and the other Disney attractions, the resorts on Disney property are the most convenient. But if you plan to visit other attractions, you should at least consider the alternatives.

Let's look at the pros and cons of staying in an on-site hotel. On the positive side, you won't need to drive, and transportation within Disney World will be free. None of the hotels is within the actual confines of the Magic Kingdom or Epcot, but transportation is usually quick and efficient. Staying on-site allows you to visit the parks in the early morning, to return to your hotel for some R&R when the park crowds are thickest, and to return to the parks in the evening when the lines are shortest.

If you have kids, they will be able to travel on their own and to stay out of trouble within Disney World. Rooms in the on-site resorts are large and can as a rule accommodate up to five persons (villas sleep six or seven). Built with families in mind, the rooms offer cable television with the Disney Channel and a channel providing the latest updates on special daily events.

The thrill—especially for younger children—of knowing you are actually living in Disney World may in itself be worth staying here. The hotels offer many of their own special events such as theme dinner shows and breakfasts at which Disney cartoon characters come to entertain the kids. You don't need to stay in these hotels to enjoy these special programs, but it's nice to have them only an elevator ride or a short walk away.

As a Disney guest, you get first rights to tee-off times at the busy golf courses and you are able to call in advance to make hard-to-get reservations at any of the fine restaurants in Epcot Center. Outsiders can make reservations only in person in the park on the day they wish to dine.

As an on-site guest, you also get a transportation pass, and with proper authorization it will allow you to charge most meals and purchases throughout WDW.

On the negative side, hotels with comparable facilities tend to cost more on Disney property than off. You may think that by staying at a Disney hotel you'll get discounts on multiple-day passports. This is little more than a promotional ploy—unless you consider a savings of a few dollars on hundreds of dollars worth of passports a significant discount. Whatever small savings you may realize will be undercut by the higher cost of staying in an on-site property.

Furthermore, Disney World—family vacationland that it is—is packed with children, and couples may prefer a more relaxed atmosphere in which to spend the night (of course some off-site properties are just as crowded). Large conventions can create a less than ideal environment for both families and couples. Of course, if complete peace and quiet are what you're after, you should be thinking of another vacation altogether.

It is true that to the cost of an off-site hotel must be added to the expense of transportation to Disney World, but shuttle service is frequent, convenient, and—if your family is small—relatively cheap.

Reservations

All on-site accommodations may be booked through the Walt Disney World Central Reservations Office, Box 10100, Suite 300, Lake Buena Vista, FL 32830, tel. 407/W–DISNEY. Reservations must often be made several months in advance and sometimes, for the best rooms during high season, a year in advance. There are always cancellations, of course, so it's worth trying even at the last minute. Keep in mind that Delta Airlines (tel. 800/221–1212) has many rooms allotted to it for its travel packages, so check with Delta, too. Visitors on a tight budget should be aware that many hotels (and attractions) offer discounts up to 40% from September to mid-December.

If the on-site resorts are full, Central Reservations will automatically try to book a place for you at one of the Walt Disney World Village Hotel Plaza hotels. Be sure to tell them exactly what you are looking for. You must give a deposit for your first night's stay within three weeks of making your reservation, and you can get a refund if you cancel at least five days before your scheduled stay.

Land packages, including admissions tickets, car rentals, and hotels either on or off Disney property, can be made through **Walt Disney Travel Co.** (1675 Buena Vista Dr., Lake Buena Vista, FL 32830, tel. 407/828–3255).

Land/air packages, with accommodations both on and off Disney property, can be booked through **Disney Reservation Service** (tel. 800/828–0228).

Ratings

The most highly recommended properties are indicated by a star ★. Rates usually include the price of two children under 18.

Category	Cost*
Very Expensive	over $150
Expensive	$120–$150
Moderate	$65–$120
Inexpensive	under $65

double room; add 9% for taxes

Disney-Owned Hotels

Visitors have a choice of staying at (1) hotels owned and operated by Disney, (2) hotels that are privately owned but that are located on Disney property, and (3) hotels in the Orlando area.

Let's look at the Disney-run hotels first. In brief, the **Contemporary** is perhaps the busiest resort—the one that is most crowded with children and conventioneers. Yet it is also the center of action, with the most entertainment, shops, and restaurants.

The **Polynesian Village** is the most popular, particularly with families and couples. It has a relaxed environment with low, tropical buildings and walking paths along the Seven Seas Lagoon. It can be difficult to find a place to be alone, however.

The charm of the **Grand Floridian** will survive the crowds. The waterfront location makes it particularly attractive.

The most relaxed and low-key of the hotels is the **Disney Inn.** It is the smallest, and, because it is between two golf courses, it is the quietest.

The **Caribbean Beach Resort** is the low-cost option for those guests who want the convenience of being on Disney property without the high prices (rooms start at $69 a night).

Disney's Village Resort, formerly the Resort Villas, is especially attractive for families or groups of two or more couples. There are four different types of villas in relatively isolated woodland settings.

Least formal are the completely equipped trailer and camp sites in the even more wooded **Fort Wilderness Campground Resort**.

Four new hotels will be added by the end of 1992. Already open is the **Disney Yacht Club** and the **Disney Beach Club,** which, combined with the privately owned Walt Disney World Dolphin and Walt Disney World Swan, make up the Epcot Center resorts. **Port Orleans** opened in the summer of 1991 between Epcot and Disney Village Marketplace. Port Orleans will be joined in 1992 by **Dixie Landings** to provide 3,056 moderately priced rooms.

Reservations sometimes become available at the last minute. For same-day reservations, phone each Disney property directly. For advance reservations call 407/W–DISNEY.

Hotels and Resorts   **Contemporary Resort.** The futuristic monorail runs right through the middle of this gigantic A-frame hotel, making visitors feel they have truly arrived in Tomorrowland. But once inside the space station of an atrium, visitors find themselves back to the present, in a rather impersonal, bustling world of restaurants, lounges, and shops. Only half of the hotel's rooms are here in this 15-story tower. They are the more expensive rooms because of their spectacular views—the higher up the better. A new concierge package is available for guests staying in the 14th-floor suites. Rooms in the front are at a premium because they look out toward the Magic Kingdom, and guests can watch the sun set and the fireworks explode over Cinderella Castle. Rooms on the back side have ringside seats for the Electrical Water Pageant and sunrise through the mists of Bay Lake. The rest of the hotel's rooms are in the North and South Gardens. Tower rooms can be somewhat noisy at night—sounds rise through the crowded atrium—so if you're a light sleeper, stay in one of the quieter wings. The wings are less expensive, and overlook the hotel's pool and gardens; the best rooms overlook Bay Lake. Try to avoid rooms that look out over the parking lot, even though they may be described as having a view of the Magic Kingdom. All the rooms in the hotel have a small terrace and most of them have two queen-size beds and a small bed for one additional person to sleep—less than comfortably. You can request a room with a king-size bed and double sofa bed. Every room has a large bathroom with double

Lodging*

Budget Host Maingate East, **30**

Buena Vista Palace, **17**

Casa Rosa Inn, **25**

Cedar Lakeside, **28**

Chalet Suzanne, **32**

Comfort Inn, **21**

Days Inn Orlando Lakeside, **5**

Embassy Suites, **6**

Enclave Suites, **4**

Gold Star Inn, **30**

Grand Cypress Resort, **11**

Grosvenor Resort, **13**

Guest Quarters, **12**

Hilton, **18**

Howard Johnson, Lake Buena Vista, **16**

Hyatt Orlando, **31**

Marriot, **22**

Orlando Heritage Inn, **2**

Park Plaza, **1**

Park Suite, **8**

Peabody Orlando, **3**

Quality Suites, **29**

Raddison Inn, **7**

Raddison Inn Maingate East, **20**

Ramada Resort Maingate, **23**

Residence Inn, **26**

Royal Plaza, **14**

Sheraton Lakeside Inn, **19**

Sonesta Village, **9**

Stouffer Orlando, **10**

Travelodge Golden Triangle, **27**

Travelodge Hotel, **15**

Vistana, **24**

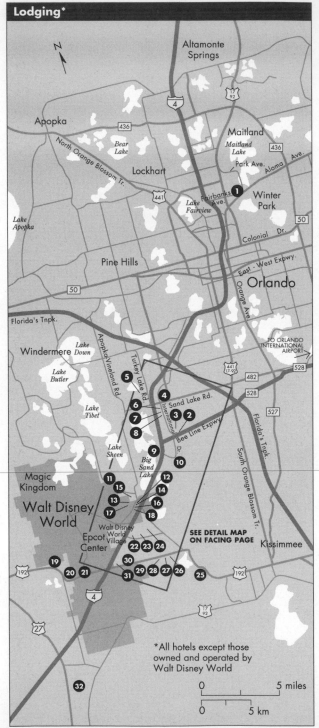

*All hotels except those owned and operated by Walt Disney World

Lodging (detail) *

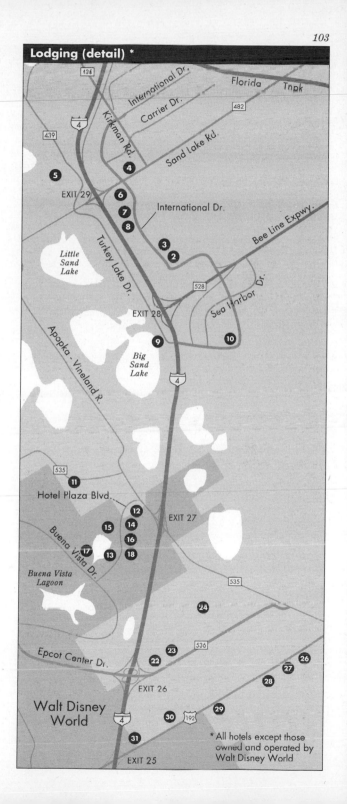

* All hotels except those owned and operated by Walt Disney World

sinks, tub, and shower. The hotel has many recreational facilities including tennis courts available at hourly rates, two swimming pools, and many water sports at its own lake marina. There is also a health club with co-ed activities in the morning and separate hours for men and women during the day. The 4th floor Grand Canyon Concourse in the tower has numerous shops selling gifts, clothing, and books. For Continental cuisine and candlelight consider the leisurely Gulf Coast Room. The fast-paced Top of the World restaurant offers nightly Broadway revues and live jazz. (Jackets required at both restaurants.) Kids will be happy to disappear into the Fiesta Fun Center, filled with every imaginable game room activity. They will also enjoy meeting the Disney characters who show up for breakfast and dinner at the Contemporary Cafe. The Contemporary is a very busy place filled with conventions and crowds, but it does have many conveniences. The monorail can take you to the Polynesian Hotel, the Magic Kingdom, and Epcot; and a motor launch can take you directly to Discovery Island and Fort Wilderness/River Country. The boat leaves from the marina behind the hotel about every 20 minutes. *WDW Central Reservations, Box 10100, Lake Buena Vista 32830, tel. 407/W–DISNEY or 407/824–1000 for same-day reservations. 1,052 rooms. AE, MC, V. Very Expensive.*

Disney Beach and Yacht Club Resort. The Yacht Club, with its lighthouse on the pier and evergreens, is a replanted slice of life from a turn-of-the-century New England seacoast. Guests enter across a wood-planked bridge to a gray clapboard, five-story, 634-room hotel with hardwood floors and gleaming brass. Equally impressive is the blue-and-white, three- to five-story, 580-room Beach Club. The croquet lawn, beachside cabanas, white sand, and hotel staff dressed in colorful 19th-century "jams" and T-shirts will have you feeling as if you are actually a part of those bygone days. Each hotel has its own restaurants and shops and shares a common public area. The public area has child-care facilities, a game arcade, a health club, and a water-recreation area that includes slides and snorkeling in a sandy-bottom lagoon stocked with Florida freshwater fish. *WDW Central Reservations, Box 10100, Lake Buena Vista 32830, tel. 407/W–DISNEY or 407/934–8000 (Beach) and 407/934–7000 (Yacht). 1,214 rooms. AE, MC, V. Very Expensive.*

Disney Inn. This is the smallest and quietest of the Disney hotels. At one time, it was called the Golf Resort and non-golfers stayed away. Others were turned off by the fact that the monorail did not stop here. The problem was easily solved by dropping the "Golf" and replacing it with the biggest name in tourism this side of Mecca, and changing "Resort" to "Inn" to signal the away-from-it-all quality of a country hostelry. The truth is that while the resort sits between two world-class golf courses and a number of golfers *do* like to stay here, the place is a great spot for couples—with or without family in tow—especially if they want to escape the more frenzied activity found at the other resorts. Rooms at the Disney Inn are slightly larger than most rooms at the other resorts. Up to five persons can sleep in two queen-size beds and a comfortable sleeper sofa. The most expensive rooms overlook the pool. If you book a room on the first floor, you can walk directly from your room to the pool; however, these rooms can be noisy at times. Less expensive rooms with views of the gardens or, better yet, the fairways are equally pleasant and quieter. As you can guess, the recreation here focuses mostly on driving and putting skills. There are three first-rate 18-hole golf courses and a 9-hole executive course. These golf facilities are open to the public, but Disney guests are accommodated first. *WDW Central Reservations, Box 10100, Lake Buena Vista 32830, tel. 407/W–DISNEY or 407/824–2200 for same-day reservations. 288 rooms. AE, MC, V. Very Expensive.*

★ **The Grand Floridian.** If you are looking for old-fashioned character, style, charm, and luxury, but also want all the conveniences of a modern hotel, the Grand Floridian Beach Resort is for you. At first glance you may think that Disney found this gilded-age masterpiece in Palm Beach or some other turn-of-the-century coastal hotspot and transported it to the shores of the Seven Seas Lagoon. But, no, the resort opened August 1, 1988. The gabled red roofing, brick chimneys, and long rambling verandahs were all built with loving attention to detail. Inside, crystal chandeliers, stained-glass domes, and ornate latticework on balconies and aviaries create the feeling of an earlier, less frenetic age. The rooms are somewhat more modern, but subdued and tasteful, with light-wood furniture and soft colors. The hotel has five bustling restaurants, two lounges, and merchandise shops featuring turn-of-the-century items. As you may expect from a beach resort, there are all sorts of water sports at the marina and enclosed boardwalk pier. Facilities include a health club, an outdoor pool, and a spa. The Grand Floridian also has its own monorail stop that links it to the Transportation and Ticket Center and the Magic Kingdom. Even the resort's monorail station carries off the elegant Victorian theme. *WDW Central Reservations, 10100 Lake Buena Vista 32830, tel. 407/W–DISNEY or 407/824–3000. 652 standard rooms; 167 smaller "attic" chambers; 69 concierge rooms; 12 suites. AE, MC, V. Very Expensive.*

Polynesian Village Resort. You are supposed to get the feeling The focal point of the resort is the Great Ceremonial House, where visitors check in. The atrium sets the tone with its lush tropical atmosphere complete with volcanic rock fountains, blooming orchids, coconut palms, and the constant rush of running water—the whole bit. You might think you were at a resort in Fiji if you didn't notice all the kids running around wearing Mickey Mouse caps. Stretching from the main building are 11 two- and three-story "longhouses," each of which carries the name of some exotic Pacific Island. All rooms offer two queen-size beds and a smaller sleeper sofa, and accommodate up to five people. Except for some second-floor rooms, all have a balcony or patio. If you don't like to walk too much and want to be near the main building with its shops and entertainment, request a room in the Bora Bora or Maui longhouses. For the best view of the Magic Kingdom and the Seven Seas Lagoon with its sandy, palm trimmed beaches, stay in the Samoa, Moorea, or Tonga. The least expensive rooms look out at the other buildings, the monorail, and the parking lot across the street. Slightly more expensive are the garden-and-pool-view rooms. Rooms overlooking the lagoon are the priciest, but they are also the most peaceful, and include a host of upgraded amenities and services that make them among the most sought after in Disney World. They, too, have a perfect view of the Electrical Water Pageant. Recreational activities center around the hotel's large sandy beach and marina, where you can rent boats for sailing, water-skiing, and fishing. If you can pull together a group of eight, you can even rent an outrigger canoe. The two swimming pools can be overrun by children; you may want to go to the beach for a dip instead. One pool is free-form and wonderfully landscaped with rocks and caverns at one end. The Polynesian Village Resort is the most popular of all Disney-owned resorts, particularly among families and honeymooners. Some 60% of the guests have been here before, so the resort must be doing something right. *WDW Central Reservations, Box 10100, Lake Buena Vista 32830, tel. 407/W–DISNEY or 824–2000 for same-day reservations. 855 rooms. AE, MC, V. Very Expensive.*

★ **Caribbean Beach Resort.** Like the Polynesian Village Resort, the Caribbean Beach Resort is made up of villages—Aruba, Barbados, Jamaica, Martinique, and Trinidad—all two-story buildings on a 42-acre tropical lake. Each village has its own swimming pool, laundry facility, and stretch of white-sand beach. Bridges over the lake connect the mainland with Parrot Cay, a one-acre island featuring footpaths, bike paths, and children's play areas. There is a 500-seat food court and an adjoining 200-seat lounge. Check-in is at the Custom House, off Buena Vista Drive. *WDW Central Reservations, 10100 Lake Buena Vista 32830, tel. 407/W–DISNEY or 407/934–3400. 1,200 one-bedroom units. AE, MC, V. Moderate.*

Disney's Village Resort

There are a few good reasons why you may prefer the Village Resort's Villas to the WDW hotels.

- You are visiting Disney with your family or with other couples and you want to stay together and avoid the expense of separate rooms.
- You enjoy the convenience of having your own kitchen and would like to save money by preparing some of your own meals.
- You don't like big, busy hotels but you appreciate the amenities of a resort.

There are five clusters of villas, each with its own character and ambience. Though they are not quite as plush as rooms in the resort hotels, they are more spacious. Since the villas are not on the monorail, transportation to the parks can be slow, and to get around within the village you may want to use your car or a rented bike or golf cart. On the positive side, you have immediate access to great golf, great fishing, shopping, and an active nightlife. Check-in for resort villas is at the new Village Resort reception center. *WDW Central Reservations, 10100 Lake Buena Vista 32830, tel. 407/W–DISNEY or 407/827–1100 for same-day reservations. All accept AE, MC, V.*

One- and Two-Bedroom Villas. They were originally built as the Vacation Villas, but—thank goodness—were refurbished in 1986. Each unit has complete living facilities with equipped kitchens and either one or two bedrooms. The one-bedroom villas have a king-size bed in one room and a queen-size sofa bed in the living room (accommodating up to four). The two-bedroom units (accommodating up to six) have either a king-size bed or two twins in each bedroom, and a living-room sofa bed. There are two outdoor pools at the Vacation Villas. *139 one-bedroom units, 87 two-bedroom units. AE, MC. Very Expensive.*

Club Suite Villas. These are the smallest and the least memorable of the villas—and also the least expensive. Built of cedar, they have one bedroom, a sofa bed, a wet bar, but no kitchens—the only villas that don't. Their size and ambience reflect the needs of the business people attending meetings at the nearby WDW Conference Center. There are a few Deluxe Club Suites that sleep six and have Jacuzzis. Facilities include two outdoor pools, a small game room, a playground, and boat rentals. *61 units. Expensive–Very Expensive.*

Two-Bedroom Villas. These villas are built of cedar, like those at Club Suite, but they are more tastefully decorated and very spacious. All have two bedrooms and a full loft, accommodating up to six. They were formerly known as the Fairway Villas because the property is surrounded by several fairways of the Lake Buena Vista Golf Course. Guests may use pools at the Villa Recreation Center or Walt Disney World Village Clubhouse. *64 units. Expensive–Very Expensive.*

Three-Bedroom Villas. If you really want to get away from it all, this is the place to stay. Isolated within a peaceful, heavily wooded area, these curious "treehouse" villas stand on stilts. You won't exactly feel like Tarzan and Jane in these bungalows, but you may hear some howls late at night. Predictably, this out-of-the-way little forest retreat is popular among young couples. All treehouses accommodate six and have two bedrooms with queen-size beds and a third bedroom with a double bed, kitchen and breakfast bar, living room, and two bathrooms. The third bedroom is on a lower level. There is also a utility room with washer/dryer. Guests can use nearby pools at the Villa Recreation Center or Walt Disney World Village Clubhouse. *60 units. Very Expensive.*

Fort Wilderness. If you want to rough it, stay here among 730 acres of woodland, streams, small lakes, and plenty of water activities along the southeastern edge of Bay Lake, at the northern edge of Disney World property. You can rent a 42-foot-long trailer (accommodating up to six) or a 35-foot trailer (accommodating up to four). Both types have one bedroom, a bath, a full kitchen, air-conditioning, heat, and daily housekeeping services. The trailer sites are spread over 80 forested acres. For those who are more serious about getting in touch with the great outdoors, there are campsites spread across 21 areas. Some are for visitors' own trailers, complete with electrical outlets, outdoor charcoal grills, private picnic tables, water, and waste disposal. Full maid service is available. There are also tent sites with water and electricity but not sewage. The most expensive sites (100 through 700) are nearest the lake. The least expensive (1600 through 1900) are far from the lake in denser vegetation. If there's bargain lodging at WDW, this is it. Each site accommodates up to 10 people. The campground has its own beach, swimming pools, volleyball and tennis courts, and all sorts of boats for rent. Fort Wilderness also offers a huge water playground called River Country, with raft rides, rope swings, a winding water slide, and a huge heated pool. Nearby, in the middle of Bay Lake, is Discovery Island, a nature preserve with more than 60 species of animals and rare birds amidst hundreds of varieties of exotic flowers, plants, and trees. You can get a boat to the island from Fort Wilderness. *WDW Central Reservations, Box 10100, Lake Buena Vista 32830, tel. 407/W–DISNEY, or same-day reservations 407/824–2900. Trailers, moderate; campsites, inexpensive.*

Other Hotels in Walt Disney World

Other than the resorts that are actually Disney-owned, the two new hotels at Epcot and the seven hotels at Hotel Plaza are the most popular among visitors to Walt Disney World. This is because the properties publicize themselves as "official Walt Disney World hotels" and offer many of the same benefits. These hotels are not owned by Disney. They were invited to establish themselves on Disney property and they pay for the privilege. Disney does keep a close eye on them, however, to ensure that they maintain certain standards. Because these hotels are on Disney property there is a premium on rooms and rates are somewhat inflated compared to what you can find off Disney property. Many Disney fans believe, however, that the benefits of staying in these hotels make it worthwhile. You decide.

- You can avoid box-office lines at Magic Kingdom, Epcot, and Disney-MGM by buying tickets at your hotel. However, you can also send for these tickets before leaving home or purchase them at the airport.
- You can make telephone reservations for restaurants and dinner shows in Disney World in advance of the general public.
- You can use the tennis and golf facilities.
- The Hotel Plaza resorts are all part of an attractively landscaped complex. Each has its own restaurants and lounges, and all are within walking distance of the popular Walt Disney World Shopping Village, a pleasant outdoor mall filled with gift shops and restaurants.
- The Epcot Center hotels, which are also attractively landscaped, have their own restaurants and lounges. Each hotel is within walking distance of Disney-MGM or Epcot.
- All nine hotels are convenient. Buses connect Epcot Center hotels with the Magic Kingdom, and Disney-MGM and Epcot can be reached on foot or by tram. From Hotel Plaza there is bus service to Epcot, Disney-MGM, and the Magic Kingdom's TTC. So if half the family wants to spend the afternoon in one of the parks and the other half wants to go back to the hotel swimming pool, it's easy.

You can call each hotel's toll-free number for reservations, or you can book rooms at any of them through the **Walt Disney World Central Reservations Office** (CRO), Box 10100, Lake Buena Vista, FL 32830, tel. 407/W–DISNEY. Delta Airline offers reservations at these hotels for discount prices in their package deals.

Epcot Center Resorts

★ **Walt Disney World Dolphin.** From a distance, this hotel gives the impression of whispered whimsy, but as you get closer, it shouts for recognition as another Disney landmark. Two 55-foot sea creatures atop each end of the hotel, with a 27-story pyramid in between, make this Sheraton-operated hotel the tallest structure in Walt Disney World. A waterfall cascades down the building's exterior from seashell to seashell and then into a 56-foot wide clamshell supported by giant dolpins sculptures. In keeping with the tropical Florida landscape, the building's facade is coral and turquoise and covered with a mural of giant banana leaves. Rooms are furnished colorfully, and amenities include an in-room safe, minibar, and a large vanity area. The best rooms overlook Epcot with a stunning view of IllumiNations. The 12th–18th Tower floors feature special registration and concierge services. Hotel facilities include multilingual concierge service, 7 restaurants, health club, game room, eight tennis courts, shops, youth hotel, beauty salon, car rental, airlines desk, and swimming in regular pools, a grotto, or a lake with a white-sand beach. Complimentary transportation connects the hotel to all the Disney attractions. While inside, be sure to note architect Michael Graves's touches of fancy inside: monkey chandeliers and the palm tree column benches. Even the elevators are a treat. *1500 Epcot Resort Blvd., Lake Buena Vista 32830, tel. 407/934–4000. 1,509 rooms (140 suites and 185 tower rooms). AE, DC, MC, V. Very Expensive.*

Walt Disney World Swan. Connected by a covered causeway with the Dolphin, the Swan is 12 stories high with two seven-story wings. Two 45-foot swans grace the rooftop. The exterior of the hotel is painted in aquamarine and coral. Inside the lobby, in typical Michael Graves fashion, is the canopied ceiling of tall, gathered papyrus reeds and palm-frond capitals. The rooms are decorated in coral, peach, teal, and yellow floral and geometric patterns. Facilities include an in-room safe, stocked refrigerator, car rental, youth hotel, baby-sitting service, three restaurants, two lounges, a health club, heated pool, tropical grotto, a white-sand beach, eight lighted tennis courts, and shops. *1200 Epcot Resort Blvd., Lake Buena Vista 32830, tel. 407/934–3000 or 800/248–SWAN or 800/228–3000. 713 rooms (45 concierge rooms on 11th, 12th floors). AE, DC, MC, V. Very Expensive.*

Hotel Plaza

The formal name of this area is Walt Disney World Village Hotel Plaza at Lake Buena Vista, but most people refer to it simply as Hotel Plaza.

To reach Lake Buena Vista Village, take I–4 west to the exit for Rte. 535, clearly marked Walt Disney World Village, Lake Buena Vista. Turn right, and at the first stoplight take a left into the Village. You will be on Hotel Plaza Blvd. Hotels line both sides of the street.

Hotels and Resorts **Buena Vista Palace and Palace Suite Resort at Walt Disney World Village.** This is the largest of the Lake Buena Vista hotels, with one of its towers soaring 27 stories. When you enter its lobby, the hotel seems smaller and quieter than its bold modern exterior and sprawling parking lots might suggest. Don't be fooled. You have entered on the third floor; when you head down to the ground level, you'll see just how large this place truly is. In 1989, $2 million was spent redecorating guest rooms in the Palace's main hotel; a $15 million project, including the addition of a 200-suite hotel with landscaped walkways connecting it to the original hotel, was scheduled to be completed by the end of 1991. Facilities at the resort include a health club, three heated swimming pools, four tennis courts, a beauty salon, a game room, gift shops, 10 restaurants and lounges, Disney tickets, airline assistance, and a complete business center with translation and secretarial service and fax. *The Outback,* an Australian-themed restaurant, serves steaks, lobsters, and 99 varieties of beer. Next door is a lively nightclub called *Laughing Kookaburra. Top of the Palace Lounge,* on the top floor, is a good perch for watching the sun set and Epcot Center's nightly bath in colored lights and lasers. Also on the top floor is the formal *Arthur's 27* (*see* Chapter 7) restaurant. Each room has its own small patio and a push-button Mickey Mouse telephone. Rooms on the upper floors are more expensive; the best ones look out toward Epcot. Ask for a room in the main tower to avoid the late-night noise that reverberates through the atrium from the nightclub. The suites each have private balconies, living room/parlors with sleeper sofas, and dining areas with appliances. The bedrooms come with one king- or two queen-size beds. *1900 Lake Buena Vista Dr., Lake Buena Vista 32830, tel. 407/827–2727 or 800/327–2990 or in FL, 800/432–2920. 1,029 rooms. AE, DC, MC, V. Expensive–Very Expensive.*

★ **Hilton at Walt Disney World Village.** The Hilton is generally considered the top hotel in the Village. It is also one of the most expensive. In contrast to the unimpressive facade, interiors are richly decorated with brass and glass, and softened with tasteful carpets. Guest rooms sparkle. Rooms are not huge, but they are cozy and contemporary, with high-tech amenities. All are the same size, with a king-size bed, two double beds, or two queen-size beds. The most expensive rooms have views of the Shopping Village and lake. Also desirable are rooms overlooking the pool. Although all rooms are the same size, they vary dramatically in price by location and floor, as well as by season, but they were all refurbished in 1990. Keep in mind that if you book a room at the lowest rate—on a lower floor with a mediocre view—the check-in clerk can assign you to a better room if one is available, at an extra charge of $45. The Towers level on the 9th and 10th floors features 84 luxurious guest rooms and suites, separate checkin and checkout, a concierge, private lounge, complimentary Continental breakfast each morning, cocktails and hors d'oeuvres in the late afternoon, plush bathrobes, and morning newspapers. The Hilton provides a service that many parents will consider indispensable—a Youth Hotel for children 4–12. It has full-time supervisors for its playroom, a large-screen television (with Disney Channel, of course), a six-bed dormitory, and scheduled meals. The Youth Hotel is open daily from 4:30 PM to midnight. The cost is $4 an hour. Other facilities include two swimming pools, a health club, two lighted tennis courts, several outdoor and indoor bars and restaurants, including the popular *American Vineyards,* serving New American cuisine. *1751 Hotel Plaza Blvd., Lake Buena Vista 32830, tel. 407/827–4000 or 800/445–8667. 813 rooms. AE, MC, V. Expensive–Very Expensive.*

Guest Quarters. This hotel has suites that consist of a comfortable living-room area and a separate bedroom with either two double beds or a king-size bed. With a sofa bed in the living room, a suite can accommodate up to six people, but certainly not all comfortably. The arrangement is convenient for small families who want to avoid the hassle of cots and the expense of two separate rooms. Each unit has a television in each room (including a small one in the bathroom!), a stocked refrigerator, a wet bar, a coffeemaker, and, on request, a microwave oven. The hotel attracts a quiet family crowd and few of the noisy conventioneers you can expect to find at larger, splashier properties. Facilities include a whirlpool spa, heated pools, two tennis courts, a game room, and a children's play area. The terrace restaurant and bar are fine for the complimentary buffet breakfasts but you will probably want to drink and dine elsewhere. *2305 Hotel Plaza Blvd., Lake Buena Vista 32830, tel. 407/934–1000 or 800/424–2900. 229 units. AE, DC, MC, V. Expensive–Very Expensive.*

Royal Plaza. From the lobby, this hotel seems a bit dated in comparison to the slick, modern hotels in the neighborhood. But the extremely casual, lively atmosphere makes it quite popular among families with young kids and teenagers. Rooms, each with a balcony, are generous in size, the best ones overlooking the pool. If you have any interest in sleeping late or napping in the afternoon, make sure your room isn't too close to the ground floor. The hotel has several restaurants and bars, a few shops, a hair salon, four lighted tennis courts, sauna, pool, and putting green. *Memory Lane*, is a new revue of American music accompanied by a four-course dinner at 6 and 9 PM daily except Monday that costs $26.95 for adults and $19.95 for children 3–11. **The Giraffe**, a nightclub featuring dancing to Top 40 hits, is open until 3 AM. *1905 Hotel Plaza Blvd., Lake Buena Vista 32830, tel. 407/828–2828 or 800/248–7890. 397 rooms. AE, DC, MC, V. Expensive–Very Expensive.*

Howard Johnson, Lake Buena Vista. This is not the handsomest hotel on the block, but it is one of the most reasonably priced, as children under 18 stay free. Though somewhat charmless, with a white formica lobby and a lackluster 14-story atrium, the hotel is popular with young couples and senior citizens. There are two heated pools, a kiddie pool, a game room, and an upgraded Howard Johnson's restaurant that's open 24 hours. *1805 Hotel Plaza Blvd., Lake Buena Vista 32830, tel. 407/828–8888 or 800/654–2000; in FL, 800/FLORIDA; in NY, 800/822–3950. 323 rooms. AE, DC, MC, V. Moderate–Very Expensive.*

Travelodge Hotel. The hotel was recently refurbished, so the minibars and queen-size beds, the rooms are unexceptional. The pool, playground, and game room are popular with kids. The hotel sponsors nightly entertainment in its Tower Club, on the 18th floor, overlooking Walt Disney World. *2000 Hotel Plaza Blvd., Lake Buena Vista 32830, tel. 407/828–2424, in FL, 800/423–1022, outside FL, 800/348–3765. 325 rooms. AE, DC, MC, V. Expensive.*

Grosvenor Resort. This attractive hotel is probably the best deal in the neighborhood, with a wealth of facilities and comfortable rooms for a fair price. The former Americana Dutch Resort, it has been completely refurbished in British-colonial style. Public areas are spacious, with high molded ceilings and columns, warm cheerful colors, and plenty of natural light. *Baskerville's* serves Continental fare and Sherlock Holmes memorabilia. A homey little pub called *Moriarity's* has live entertainment. Recreational facilities are geared toward the active life and include two heated pools, two lighted tennis courts, racquetball, shuffleboard, basketball and volleyball courts, a children's playground, and a game room. Rooms are average in size, but colorfully decorated, with a refrigerator/bar and a videocassette player. In the lobby you can rent movies for the VCR or cameras to make your own videos. *1850 Hotel Plaza Blvd., Lake Buena Vista 32830, tel. 407/828–4444 or 800/624–4109. 629 rooms. AE, DC, MC, V. Moderate–Expensive.*

The Orlando Area

The number of hotels, motels, and resorts in the Orlando area is simply astounding. Just about every American hotel chain has at least one hotel in the vicinity.

Since its birth as a tourist mecca, Orlando's hotel industry has grown continuously. With more than 76,000 hotel rooms, Orlando leads the country in accommodations. New hotels of all sizes and varieties seem to open every day. In the early days of Disney World, the large hotels were limited primarily to Disney property, but more recently there has been a boom in huge resorts catering largely to business convention crowds. These have spread to International Drive. Whether you're staying in the inexpensive Kissimmee area (with its smaller hotels), along International Drive (with both large and small hotels), or anywhere around the Disney Maingate (around the northernmost entrance, just off I–4), nearly all hotels provide frequent transportation to and from Walt Disney World. What matters most is that you choose a hotel within your price range, where you can be comfortable.

International Drive

The International Drive area, referred to by locals as "I Drive" and formally labeled "Florida Center," is a main drag for all sorts of hotels, restaurants, and shopping malls. As you head north along the Drive, the hotels get cheaper, the restaurants turn into fast food joints, and malls translate into factory outlets. The southern end of the Drive is classier, but the northern end may be more congenial to your budget—particularly if all you need is a place to put your head at night.

You will be hard-pressed to find any structure around here older than you are, even if you are a teenager, since the area has been built up mostly in the last 15 years as an alternative to the Disney properties. For those not exclusively interested in Disney World, the Drive is a convenient point of departure for Orlando's countless other attractions. The Drive immediately parallels I–4 (at exits 28, 29, and 30), so a few minutes' drive north puts you in downtown Orlando, while a few minutes south on I–4 puts you in Disney World.

The International Drive area showcases such local attractions as Sea World, Universal Studios, the labyrinth water-slide park, Wet 'n Wild, and many popular dinner shows. Many veteran Orlando visitors consider International Drive the territory's most comfortable home base, featuring some of the best hotels around.

Hotels and Resorts **Peabody Orlando.** From afar, the Peabody looks like a high rise office building. Don't let its austere exterior scare you away! Once inside, you will discover a very impressive, handsomely designed hotel. If you ignore the soaring numbers in the elevators and the sweeping view from your room, you will never know you are in a skyscraping, 27-story hotel. The Peabody's lobby has rich marble floors and fountains, and the entire hotel is decorated with modern art, giving it much color and flair. The rooms with the best views face Disney World and a sea of orange trees that extends as far as the eye can see. If you want to be pampered, stay in the Peabody Clubs on the top three floors and enjoy special concierge service. The hotel was built by the owners of the famous Peabody Hotel in Memphis, a landmark there since the 1920s. Following in the tradition of the Memphis Peabody, the Orlando hotel has as its symbol a mallard duck. Each morning at 11, ducks (yes, real ones) waddle in a parade down an elevator, through the lobby on a red carpet to spend the day around a marble fountain. They march back at 5 PM. The Peabody has a pool, a health club, and four lighted tennis courts. There are also two fine restaurants, *Capriccio's* for Italian fare and *Dux* for Continental cuisine. There is also a 24-hour 1950s-style diner, the *Beeline*. Located across the street from the Orlando Convention/Civic Center, the hotel attracts concert performers from across the street and conventioneers. *9801 International Dr., Orlando 32819, tel. 407/352–4000 or 800/PEABODY. 891 rooms. AE, DC, MC, V. Expensive–Very Expensive.*

Sonesta Villa Resort Orlando. The Sonesta, located off I–4 near International Drive, is a string of multi-unit townhouses on a lakefront. Following the lead of the all-suite hotels, the Sonesta "villas" consist of small apartments, some of which are bilevel with a fully equipped kitchenette, dining room/living room area, small patio, and bedroom. The units are comfortable and homey, each with its private, ground-floor entrance. One bonus of staying at the Sonesta is the outdoor facilities, including tennis courts, mini health club, swimming pool, and whirlpools convenient to each villa. Guests can sail and water-ski on the lake or offer themselves to the sun on a sandy beach. There is a restaurant and bar, but the only action is the nightly outdoor barbecue buffet. If you want to cook at "home" but are too busy to go shopping, the hotel offers a grocery delivery service. Laundry, however, is self-service. *10000 Turkey Lake Rd., Orlando 32819, tel. 407/352–8051 or 800/SONESTA. 384 units. AE, DC, MC, V. Expensive.*

Stouffer Orlando Resort. From the same people who brought the French bread pizza and Lean Cuisine to the frozen section of your grocery store comes an even more palatable product—the Stouffer Hotel. This first-rate resort was originally the Wyndham Hotel Sea World, until it was sold to the Stouffer chain in 1987. Located directly across the street from Sea World, this bulky, 10-story building looks more like a Federal Reserve Bank than a comfortable hotel. When you enter, you have stepped into what is billed as the largest atrium lobby in the world. Longer than a football field, it takes up the entire core of the building and is ornately landscaped with waterfalls, goldfish ponds, palm trees, glass elevators, and a large, hand-carved, gilded Victorian aviary from Venice, complete with exotic birds. Facilities include six lighted tennis courts, a swimming pool, a whirlpool, a child-care center, a game room, and access to an 18-hole golf course. On the second floor are a Nautilus-equipped fitness center and a beauty salon where you can work off or hide the effects of dinner you may have had at either of two commendable hotel restaurants, *Haifeng* and *Atlantis*. The Stouffer also has its own antiques and gift shops. It is nice to be greeted with a glass of champagne when you register, but the size of the guest rooms is even more welcoming. They are all large and spacious. The most expensive rooms face the atrium, but if you are a light sleeper, ask for an outside room and avoid the music and party sounds of conventioneers rising through the atrium. *6677 Sea Harbor Dr., Orlando 32821, tel. 407/351–*

5555 or 800/HOTELS–1. 778 rooms. AE, DC, MC, V. Expensive.

Embassy Suites Hotel at Plaza International. The concept of the and the Embassy Suites, a chain hotel, was the first to offer it. All suites have both a bedroom and a full living room equipped with wet bar, refrigerator, desk, pull-out sofa, and two TVs. It is a comfortable and economical arrangement, somewhat less expensive than a single room in the top-notch hotels. Because the bedroom can be closed off, it is ideal for small families. The core of the hotel is a wide atrium. It is not nearly as large as the atrium at the Stouffer, but it is much cozier, with a relaxing lounge and pianist as its centerpiece. The hotel has an indoor and an outdoor pool, an exercise room with Jacuzzi and sauna, a steam room, and a game room, but none of the other recreational facilities of the larger hotels. *8250 Jamaican Ct., Orlando 32819, tel. 407/345–8250 or 800/327–9797. 246 rooms. AE, DC, MC, V. Moderate–Expensive.*

The Enclave Suites at Orlando. This all-suite hotel is less a hotel than a condominium complex with three 10-story buildings surrounding an office, a restaurant, and a recreation area. The suites are like apartments, offering significantly more space than the other all-suite hotels. They contain full kitchens, living rooms, and small terraces. For about the same price as a room in a big, fancy hotel, you can have two bedrooms and all the amenities of home—with accommodations for up to six people. The arrangement is ideal for families or small groups of friends who want to get away from the hotel hustle. The single suites are great for couples. Weekly rates offer additional savings. Facilities include one indoor and two outdoor pools, a Jacuzzi and sauna, an exercise room, a lighted tennis court, a children's play area, and a restaurant called the *Enclave Beach Cafe* that is popular with local yuppies. *6165 Carrier Dr., Orlando 32819, tel. 407/351–1155 or 800/457–0077. 321 suites. AE, DC, MC, V. Moderate–Expensive.*

Orlando Heritage Inn. If you are looking for a simple, small hotel with reasonable rates but plenty of deliberate charm, the Heritage is the place to stay. Located next to the towering Peabody, this inn creates the atmosphere of Victorian-style Florida, complete with reproduction turn-of-the-century furnishings, rows of French windows and brass lamps, and a smattering of genuine 19th-century antiques. The guest rooms are decorated with a colonial accent—lace curtains on double French doors, folk art prints on the walls, and quilted bed covers. The hotel has a small saloon-type lounge, and there is a dinner theater in the large Victorian rotunda several nights a week. With the exception of a swimming pool, there are few facilities. The whole place has a kitschy quaintness, in contrast to the area's other hotels, and a staff that is strong on southern hospitality. *9861 International Dr., Orlando 32819, tel. 407/352–0008, in FL, 800/282–1890, or outside FL, 800/447–1890. 150 rooms. AE, DC, MC, V. Moderate.*

Park Suite. Park Suite is another all-suite hotel, similar to the Embassy Suites, but with a southern flavor. The lobby has an old-fashioned feeling to it, with marble floors and pillars, hanging lamps, and ceiling fans. When you step into the hotel's atrium you are struck by the faint, humid smell of the Deep South, which comes from its tropical gardens and mossy rock fountains. The suites are comfortable, with all the amenities of the Embassy Suites, plus a microwave oven. The difference between these two all-suite hotels is that the Embassy is brassy modern while the Park, with its ceramic tile walkways and brick arches, exudes a sense of the past. Also, the rates at the Park are slightly lower. The Park has a restaurant and bar, exercise equipment, and a fancy indoor pool with whirlpool, steam room, and sauna. *8978 International Dr., Orlando 32819, tel. 407/352–1400 or 800/432–7272. 245 suites. AE, DC, MC, V. Moderate.*

Radisson Inn & Aquatic Center. If you want to get in shape while visiting Orlando but want to avoid fancy resort prices, this is the place for you. Radisson is a big, modern, moderately priced hotel offering comfortable rooms (the best ones face the pool), but what makes it truly special are its outstanding athletic facilities. The hotel has a fine outdoor pool, but for those who are serious about swimming there is also an indoor Aquatic Center with an Olympic-size swimming and diving pool. The center was built for competitive swimming and diving events and has a high-tech Human Performance Lab for personal health assessment. Other hotel facilities include a complete Nautilus center with weights and aerobicycles; tennis, raquetball, and handball courts; a jogging track; aerobics and swimmercise classes; and plenty more, including access to a local country club for golf. *8444 International Dr., Orlando 32819, tel. 407/345–0505 or 800/333–3333. 300 rooms. AE, DC, MC, V. Moderate.*

Days Inn Orlando/Lakeside. Among the budget motels in the International Drive area, this Days Inn is tops because of its location on the shores of Spring Lake, across I–4 from International Drive. The facility has three pools, picnic areas, and playgrounds. The beach is perfect for sunning, swimming, water sports, or volleyball and is complimented by a Tiki bar. Suites with coffee maker, microwave, and refrigerator are available. A shuttle service takes guests to the main attractions for a nominal fee. This motel upholds the Days Inn trademark of allowing children of guests to eat free in its restaurants. *7335 Sand Lake Rd., Orlando 32819, tel. 407/351–1900 or 800/777–DAYS. 691 rooms. AE, DC, MC, V. Inexpensive.*

Maingate Resorts

Maingate refers to an area full of large hotels unaffiliated with Walt Disney World but clustered around its northernmost entrance just off I–4. They are mostly resort hotels on sprawling properties, catering to Walt Disney World vacationers. All are quality hotels with a resort sameness one can find the world over. But in size and price, however, they do vary. As a simple rule of thumb, the bigger the resort and the more extensive the facilities, the more you can expect to pay. If you're looking for a clean, modern room, you cannot go wrong with any of them. All are equally convenient to Walt Disney World, but one may emphasize a particular recreational activity over others. Where you stay may depend on how much time you plan to spend at your hotel or on which stroke—drive or backhand—you feel needs most improving.

Hotels and Resorts **Grand Cypress Resort.** If you were to ask someone familiar with the Orlando area which resort is the most spectacular, few would hesitate to name the Grand Cypress. The resort property is so extensive—over 1,500 acres—that guests need a trolley system to get around. There is virtually every activity you can imagine at a resort: a dozen tennis courts, boats of all shapes and varieties, scenic bicycling and jogging trails, a full health club, dozens of horses, a 600,000-gallon triple-level swimming pool fed by 12 cascading waterfalls, a 45-acre Audubon nature reserve, 45 holes of Jack Nicklaus—designed golf, and a golfing academy for high-tech analysis of your game. Guests have a choice of the 750-room Hyatt Regency Grand Cyprus or another 150 rooms at The Villas of Grand Cyprus. The hotel itself is exactly what you would expect from a first-class Hyatt resort, with a 12-story glass atrium filled with tropical plants and classical Asian paintings and sculptures. The rooms are unmemorable but very spacious, and the service is attentive. The best views look out over the pool and the rest of the hotel property. For fine dining, there is *Hemingway's*, specializing in sea food, and *La Coquina*, an upscale French place, both of which are excellent. This huge resort has just one drawback: the king-size conventions that it commonly attracts. *1 Grand Cypress Blvd., Orlando 32819, tel. 407/239-1234 or 800/233-1234. 750 rooms. AE, DC, MC, V. Very Expensive.*

Marriott Orlando World Center. To refer to this Marriott as massive would be an understatement. It has 1,503 rooms on 28 floors, and luxurious villas, called the Royal Palms and the Sabal Palms, available for weekly rental. An 18-hole golf course, a dozen tennis courts, a full health club, four swimming pools (one of them the largest in the state), 13 restaurants and bars—this is just the beginning of a list of facilities. The lobby is a huge, opulent atrium, and the rooms are clean and comfortable. The only negative aspects are the overwhelming size and the hundreds of conventioneers. *8701 World Center Dr., Orlando 32821, tel. 407/239-4200 or 800/228-9290. 1,503 rooms. AE, DC, MC, V. Very Expensive.*

★ **Vistana Resort.** Anyone interested in tennis should consider staying at this peaceful resort spread over 95 beautifully landscaped acres. It is also popular with families or groups willing to share a spacious, tastefully decorated villa or town house, each with at least two bedrooms and all the facilities of home—full kitchen, living room, washer/dryer, and so on. The price may seem high, but considering the number of people each condominium-like unit can accommodate (up to six or eight), the rates can be a bargain. The 14 clay and all-weather tennis courts can be used without charge. Private or semiprivate lessons are available for every type of player. Other facilities include five heated outdoor pools and a full health club. *8800 Vistana Centre Dr., Orlando, 32821, tel. 407/239-3100 or 800/877-8787. 722 units. AE, DC, MC, V. Very Expensive.*

Hyatt Orlando Hotel. This is another very large hotel, but without the extensive resort facilities. Instead of a single towering building, the hotel consists of nine two-story buildings in four clusters. Each cluster is a community with its own heated pool, Jacuzzi, park, and playground at its center. The rooms are spacious, but otherwise unmemorable. The lobby and convention center are in a building at the center of the clusters. The lobby is vast and mall-like, with numerous shops and restaurants. One of the restaurants, the *Palm Terrace*, features a full kosher menu supervised by the Orthodox Union. There is also a very good take-out deli with great picnic snacks for those wise enough to avoid the lines and prices at amusement park fast-food stands. There are a few tennis courts, but not much else in the way of recreation. However, for busy travelers who will be spending most of their time attacking Orlando's attractions, this is a convenient, not-too-expensive headquarters. *6375 W. Irlo Bronson Memorial Hwy., Kissimmee 34746, tel. 407/396–1234 or in FL, 800/331–2003; outside FL, 800/544–7178. 924 rooms. AE, DC, MC, V. Moderate.*

★ **Ramada Resort Maingate at the Parkway.** The Ramada, with its attractive setting and competitive prices, may offer the best deal in the neighborhood. It has 3 lighted tennis courts, a swimming pool with a waterfall, a few shops and restaurants, and a delicatessen for picnickers. The rooms, like the rest of the hotel grounds, are spacious and bright, decked out in tropical and pastel colors. The best rooms, because of the view and light, face the pool. *2900 Parkway Blvd., Kissimmee 34746, tel. 407/396–7000 or 800/634–4774; in FL, 800/225–3939. 716 rooms. AE, DC, MC, V. Moderate.*

U.S. 192 Area

If you are looking for anything remotely quaint, charming, or sophisticated, move on. The U.S. 192 strip, formally called Irlo Bronson Memorial Highway and referred to as the Spacecoast Parkway, is generally known as Kissimmee; but whatever you call it, it is an avenue crammed with bargain basement motels, hotels, cheap restaurants, fast-food chains, nickel-and-dime attractions, gas stations, and mini-marts. If all you are looking for is a decent room with perhaps a few extras for a manageable price, this is your wonderland. The number of motels here is mind-boggling. It is a buyer's market, and room rates start as low as $20 a night—or lower if it is the right time of year and you can cut the right deal. But most rooms will run about $30–$70 a night, depending on the hotel's facilities and its proximity to Disney World. Among the chain hotels—Travelodge, Econolodge, Comfort Inn, Holiday Inn, Radisson, Sheraton, Best Western, and so on—are a pride of family-operated motels, many of which are run by recent immigrants: a Norwegian couple at the Viking Motel, say, or a Chinese family at the Casa Rosa.

The rooms are very basic and there is not a whole lot of difference between them. As a rule, the newer the property, the more comfortable your surroundings are likely to be. Also, the farther you are from Disney World, the lower the rates; a few minutes' drive may save you a significant amount of money. As you drive through Kissimmee, shop around for what appeals to you. Don't be bashful about going up to a registration desk and asking to see a room before you make a decision.

Hotels and Resorts **The Residence Inn.** Of the all-suite hotels on U.S. 192, this one is probably the best. It consists of a row of four-unit town houses with private stairway entrances to each suite. One side of the unit faces the highway, the other overlooks a rather attractive lake, where visitors can sail, waterski, Jet-ski, and fish. Forty of the units are penthouses, with complete kitchens, small living rooms, loft bedrooms, and even fireplaces. The other units are set up like studio apartments, but still contain full kitchens and fireplaces. Regular studio suites accommodate two people; double studios accommodate up to four. Both Continental breakfast and a grocery shopping service are complimentary. The price may seem expensive, considering the location, but there is no charge for additional guests, so you can squeeze in the whole family at no extra charge. *4786 W. Irlo Bronson Memorial Hwy., Kissimmee 34746, tel. 407/396–2056; in FL, 800/648–7408; or outside FL, 800/468–3027. 160 units. AE, DC, MC, V. Moderate–Expensive.*

Radisson Inn Maingate. The hotel, just a few minutes from WDW's front door, is a very sleek, modern building with cheerful guest rooms, large bathrooms, and plenty of extras for the price. Facilities include a swimming pool, a whirlpool, two lighted tennis courts, and a jogging trail. Not fancy, but sufficient. The best rooms are those with a view of the pool. One floor is reserved for nonsmokers. *7501 W. Irlo Bronson Memorial Hwy., Kissimmee 34746, tel. 407/396–1400 or 800/333–3333. 580 rooms. AE, DC, MC, V. Moderate.*

Sheraton Lakeside Inn. This is a comfortable but undistinguished resort-style hotel, offering quite a few recreational facilities for its price. The complex consists of 15 two-story buildings spread over 25 acres. Facilities include heated pools, wading pools for tots, paddleboats, 18 holes of miniature golf, and 4 tennis courts. There is also a seafood restaurant, a deli, and a bar. *7711 W. Irlo Bronson Memorial Hwy., Kissimmee 34746, tel. 407/239–7919; 800/325–3535; or in FL, 800/422–8250. 651 rooms. AE, DC, MC, V. Moderate.*

Quality Suites East of Maingate. This hotel, built in 1989, is an inexpensive and roomy alternative for a large family. The rooms, designed to sleep six or 10, are decorated in green and gold and come equipped with major appliances and extras like microwave, toaster, and coffee maker. A Microwave Mini Market, game room, guest laundry, heated pool, and poolside bar are located in the patio courtyard. Kids will enjoy the motel's restaurant with a toy train chugging along overhead. Nonsmoking suites are available. *5876 W. Irlo Bronson Memorial Hwy., Kissimmee 34746, tel. 407/396–8040 or 800/228–5151. 225 units. AE, D, DC, MC, V. Moderate.*

Comfort Inn Maingate. This hotel, one mile west of WDW's main entrance, offers a place to stay that is close to Disney World but not on the property and can you save a bundle. A swimming pool, game room, restaurant, a lounge, gift shop, and playground are available. Shuttle service to major attractions is available for a nominal charge. Children age 17 and under stay free. *7571 W. Irlo Bronson Memorial Hwy., Kissimmee 34746, tel. 407/396–7500 or 800/228–5150. 281 rooms. AE, DC, MC, V. Inexpensive–Moderate.*

Casa Rosa Inn. For simple motel living—no screaming kids or loud music, please—this is your place. The pink, Spanish-style motel does not have much in the way of facilities other than a little swimming pool and free in-room movies, but it is a good, serviceable place to hang your hat. *4600 W. Irlo Bronson Memorial Hwy., Kissimmee 34746, tel. 407/396–2020 or 800/432–0665. 54 rooms. AE, MC, V. Inexpensive.*

Cedar Lakeside. The Mediterranean-style motel architecture is not likely to charm you off your feet, but the staff is friendly and facilities include a swimming pool, a Jacuzzi, and a lakefront beach with picnic areas, waterskiing, and sailing. Ask for a room as close to the lake as possible. Since there's no restaurant, you may want to pay an extra $10 for a room with a kitchenette. *4960 W. Irlo Bronson Memorial Hwy., Kissimmee 34741, tel. 407/396–1376 or 800/327–0072. 200 rooms. AE, DC, MC, V. Inexpensive.*

Gold Star Inn. Clean, close, and courteous, this former Econo Lodge is for people who don't demand many extras other than a a room as close to the lake as possible. Since there's no restaurant, you may want to pay an extra $10 for a room with a kitchenette. *4960 W. Irlo Bronson Memorial Hwy., Kissimmee 34741, tel. 407/396–1376 or 800/327–0072. 200 rooms. AE, DC, MC, V. Inexpensive.*

Travelodge Golden Triangle. The surroundings are less than room has much of a view, but try to get one as close to the lake as possible to avoid highway noise. *4944 W. Irlo Bronson Memorial Hwy., Kissimmee 34746, tel. 407/396–4455; in FL 800/228–4427 or 800/432–1022. 222 rooms. AE, DC, MC, V. Inexpensive.*

Off the Beaten Track

Winter Park

Mention should be made of two hotels that are off the beaten track—close enough to be part of the immediate Orlando area, but not so close that they fit into one of our categories.

★ **Park Plaza Hotel.** Located in Orlando's very posh, established neighborhood of Winter Park, the Park Plaza is an old-fashioned wood-and-wicker Southern hotel, built in 1922. If you are in need of recreational facilities or special amenities, look elsewhere, but if you are hoping to find real southern charm and hospitality, this is perhaps the best place in the Orlando area to find it. You are as far from the world of tourism as you can get and still within a short driving distance of all the major attractions. It is a small, intimate hotel that gives you the feeling that you are a guest in somebody's home. You wake up in the morning to a newspaper under your door, for example. All of the rooms open up onto one long balcony, covered with ferns, flowers, and wicker furniture. Rooms have either one double- or queen-size bed, and come in various sizes, with views of Park Avenue or Central Park. On the first floor is one of Orlando's most popular restaurants, the *Park Plaza Gardens,* where over Continental cuisine you can see-and-be-seen by the fashionable folk of Winter Park. *307 Park Ave. S, Winter Park 32789, tel. 407/647–1072 or 800/228–7220. 27 rooms. AE, DC, MC, V. Moderate–Expensive. To get there, drive east on I–4 and exit at Fairbanks Ave. Turn right and travel for 1 mi until you reach Park Ave. The hotel is on your left.*

Lake Wales

★ **Chalet Suzanne.** You'll find this conversation piece of a hotel in orange grove territory, in what seems the middle of nowhere. A homemade billboard directs you down a country road that turns into a palm-lined drive. Cobblestone paths lead to a row of chalet-style houses and cabins, complete with balconies and thatched roofing. On one side are fields and gardens, on the other, a lake. The Chalet Suzanne is a friendly, homespun mom-and-pop operation. It has been in the Hinshaw family for generations and was turned into a country inn when family fortunes dwindled in the 1930s. The inn has been built bit-by-unlikely-bit over the years, and the furnishings range from the rare and valuable to the garage-sale special. The grounds are decorated with colorful tilework from Portugal, ironwork from Spain, pottery from Italy, and porcelain from England and

Germany. Each room has its own personality, as in the house of a rich, eccentric old uncle. Bathrooms are tiled and have old-fashioned tubs and wash basins. The most charming rooms face the lake. *U.S. 27S, Drawer AC, Lake Wales 33859, tel. 813/676–6011. 30 rooms. AE, DC, MC, V. Moderate–Expensive. To get there, either land your Cessna or Lear jet on their private airstrip, or drive. Go west on I–4 from Orlando to the Rte. 27 exit and head toward Cypress Gardens. The Chalet's billboard is past the Cypress Gardens turnoff, just after Lake Wales.*

9 Nightlife

Disney World

Broadway at the Top. This is Disney's sophisticated nighttime entertainment spot, located at the Top of the World Nightclub atop the Contemporary Resort. The spirited show runs for about an hour after each of the two nightly seatings for dinner. A cast of high-energy dancers and singers brings to life some of Broadway's greatest hits. A single price includes the show and dinner. Tax, gratuity, and alcoholic drinks are extra. *Contemporary Resort, tel. 407/W–DISNEY. Jackets required. Reservations normally necessary at least a month in advance. No smoking. Admission: $42.50 adults, $19.50 children 3–11. Seatings at 6 PM and 9:15 PM.*

Polynesian Revue and Mickey's Tropical Revue. Put on some comfortable, casual clothes and head over to the Polynesian Village Resort for an outdoor barbecue and a tropical Luau complete with fire jugglers and hula drum dancers. It's a colorful, South Pacific setting and an easy-going evening that families find relaxing and trouble-free. There are two shows nightly of the Polynesian Revue and an earlier show for children called Mickey's Tropical Revue, where Disney characters perform decked out in costumes befitting these South Seas surroundings. *Polynesian Village Resort, tel. 407/W–DISNEY. Dress: casual. Reservations necessary, usually months in advance. No smoking. Polynesian Review: $29 adults, $23 juniors 12–20, and $15 children 3–11. Seatings at 6:45 PM and 9:30 PM. Mickey's Tropical Revue: $25 adults, $20 juniors, $11 children. Seating at 4:30 PM.*

Hoop-Dee-Doo Revue. This family-entertainment dinner show may be corny but it is also the liveliest and most rollicking in Walt Disney World. A troupe of jokers called the Pioneer Hall Players stomp their feet, wisecrack, and make merry in this Western mess-hall setting. The chow consists of barbecued ribs, fried chicken, corn-on-the-cob, strawberry shortcake, and all the fixin's. There are three shows nightly at Pioneer Hall in Fort Wilderness area—not always the easiest place to get to. *Fort Wilderness Resort, tel. 407/W–DISNEY. Dress: informal. Reservations necessary, usually months in advance, but to try for same-day reservations, call 407/824–2748. No smoking inside Pioneer Hall. Admission: $32 adults, $24 juniors 12–20, $16 children 3–11. Seatings at 5, 7:30, and 10 PM.*

Pleasure Island. Similar in concept to Church Street Station, Orlando's big tourist nightlife attraction, this multitheme, six-acre entertainment complex is connected to Disney Village Marketplace and the mainland by three footbridges and gives families an opportunity to spread out and meet later. The seven nightclubs get rolling about 6:30 and close at 2; the 11 shops open at 10 AM and close at midnight or later; the five restaurants are open about 11 AM–2 AM; and a 10-screen AMC theater features matinee and evening shows, beginning at 1:30 PM. Pleasure Island changed a few nightclubs, dropped cover charges and added a nightly New Year's Eve theme complete with fireworks to bring some weeknight action to the family-oriented enterainment complex. It now costs $9.95 after 7 PM or $12 if you get the Pleasure Island/AMC combination ticket. The ticket gives you admission to all clubs. Fireworks are at midnight on Friday and Saturday, and 11 PM the rest of the week. There is no admission fee required to dine at the Empress Lilly,

Fireworks Factory, or the Portobello Yacht Club. *Pleasure Island, tel. 404/934–7781. Dress: informal. Reservations not necessary.*

Adventurers Club. The ambiance is of an exclusive private club of adventure travelers from the 1930s. But you have to stay alert to see if that trophy on the wall is actually talking to you, if the bar stool you are sitting on is actually sinking, or if the person at the next table is a guest or part of the live entertainment. *Opens at 6.30; guests under 18 must be accompanied by an adult.*

Baton Rouge Lounge. Hot jazz, frequently mixed with a lot of laughs, is featured here. *Opens at noon; guests under 18 must be accompanied by an adult.*

Cage. This club changed from Videopolis East, a high-tech, nonalcoholic club aimed at the 13–20 age group, to a club featuring progressive rock for an over-21 crowd. *Opens at 7; guests must be 21 and over.*

Comedy Warehouse. The club has evolved from a predictable troupe of comedians to an improvisational setup, with shows at 7:20, 8:40, 10, and 11 nightly, plus 12:40 AM Friday and Saturday. *Guests under 18 must be accompanied by an adult.*

Mannequins Dance Palace. Dancing to Top 40 hits is the draw in this high-tech nightclub with a revolving dance floor and special effects. Some of the mannequins are animated. *Opens at 8; guests must be 21 or older.*

Neon Armadillo Music Saloon. Live country-and-western music in a setting straight out of a southwestern saloon. *Opens at 7; guests under 18 must be accompanied by an adult.*

XZFR Rock and Roll Beach Club. Always crowded, this three-tier building combines dancing, dining, and drinking with a live band and disc jockeys who never let the action die down. *Guests under 18 must be accompanied by an adult.*

IllumiNations. You won't want to miss Epcot's grand finale, a laser show that takes place every night just before Epcot closes, along the shores of the World Showcase lagoon. It is a show unlike any other. In the middle of the lagoon, laser projections of dancing images move across screens of spraying water. Orchestral music fills the air as multicolored neon lasers streak across the sky, pulsating to the rhythms of the music. Suddenly the night lights up with brilliant fireworks, lasers play over the low-hanging smoke, and the air vibrates with the sounds of Tchaikovsky's *1812 Overture.* Projections of the Earth's continents transform Spaceship Earth into a luminescent, spinning globe. With this dramatic finale, the crowds exit as Spaceship Earth continues to "rotate." The lasers used to create these images are powerful enough to project an identical image on a golf ball up to five miles away. It is a stellar performance.

Some places around the lagoon offer much better vantage points than others for watching the laser show. The best locations are the Matsu No Ma Lounge in the Japan Pavilion, and the patios of the Rose and Crown in the United Kingdom Pavilion and Cantina de San Angel in the Mexican Pavilion. Another good spot is the World Showcase Plaza between the boat docks at the Showcase entrance, but this is often crowded with visitors who want to make a quick dash homeward after the show; if you want to join them there, claim your seat at least an hour in advance. Since the fireworks create a good deal of smoke, you will not want to be downwind, so use the old lick-the-finger test to see which way the wind is blowing, and position yourself accordingly.

The Orlando Area

Until a few years ago, Orlando's nightlife was more like that of Oskaloosa, Iowa, than of a booming tourist haven. But slowly an after-dark scene has developed, spreading farther and farther beyond the realm of Disney. Orlando entrepreneurs have now caught on that there is a fortune to be had satisfying the fun-hungry night owls who flock to this city. New night spots are opening constantly—everything from flashy discos to ballroom dancing, country-and-western saloons, Broadway dinner theaters, even medieval jousting tournaments.

The Arts

If all the fantasy starts to wear thin and you feel the need for more sophisticated entertainment, check out the local fine arts scene in *Orlando Magazine, Center Stage,* or "Calendar," which is printed every Friday in *The Orlando Sentinel.* They are all available at any newsstand. The average price of a ticket to performing arts events in the Orlando area rarely exceeds $12, and is often half that price.

Orlando has an active performing arts agenda of ballet, modern dance, classical music, opera, and theater, much of which takes place at the **Carr Performing Arts Centre** (401 Livingston St., Orlando, tel. 407/849–2020). This community auditorium presents a different play each month (Wed. through Sat., with Sun. matinees). The Broadway series features performances on the way to Broadway or current road shows.

During the school year, **Rollins College** (tel. 407/646–2233) in Winter Park has a choral concert series that is open to the public and usually free. The first week of March there is a **Bach Music Festival** (tel. 407/646–2182) that has been a Winter Park tradition for over 55 years. Also at the college is the **Annie Russell Theater** (tel. 407/646–2145), which has a regular series of productions.

The **Orange County Convention and Civic Center** (tel. 407/345–9800) on the south end of International Drive, and the **Orlando Arena** downtown (tel. 407/849–2020), play host to many big-name performing artists.

Dinner Shows

Dinner shows have become an immensely popular form of nighttime entertainment around Orlando. A set price usually buys a multiple-course dinner and a theatrical production—a totally escapist experience. The food tends to be predictable—definitely not the major attraction. Always call and make reservations in advance, especially on weekends. A lively crowd can be an asset; a show playing to a small audience can be a pathetic and embarrassing sight. What the shows lack in substance and depth they make up for in color and enthusiasm. The result is an evening of light entertainment, which kids in particular will enjoy.

Arabian Nights. This attraction features more than 60 performing horses, music, special effects, and a chariot race; keep your eyes open for a unicorn. The outside looks like an elaborate palace, but on the inside it's an arena with seating for more than 1,200 spectators. It even has a glass-enclosed sky box for private functions. Visitors sit at long tables and watch about 25 acts as they dine on four-course dinners such as prime rib or vegetarian lasagna and unlimited beer, wine, or soft drinks. A low-cholesterol chicken or whitefish dinner is available with advance reservations. *6225 W. Irlo Bronson Memorial Hwy. (U.S. 192), Kissimmee, tel. 800/553–6116; in Canada, 800/533–3615; in Orlando, 407/239–9223; in Kissimmee, 407/396–7400. Dress: casual. Reservations necessary. AE, DC, MC, V. Admission: $27.97 adults, $16.95 children 3–11.*

Mardi Gras. This recently expanded, jazzy, New Orleans–style show is the best of Orlando's dinner attractions. The set menu consists of vegetable soup, Caesar salad, chicken breast stuffed with herb dressing or a vegetarian plate, steamed broccoli, potatoes, and all the beer, wine, or soda you can drink. It is not an elaborate meal, but it is as good as one can expect from a dinner theater. A New Orleans jazz band plays during dinner, followed by a one-hour cabaret with colorful song and dance routines to rhythms of the Caribbean, Latin America, and Dixieland jazz. Although the kids are more likely to vote for the Wild West or medieval shows, adults tend to prefer Mardi Gras because it is more of a restaurant nightclub than a fantasyland. *At the Mercado Mediterranean Village, 8445 International Dr., Orlando, tel. 407/351–5151 or 800/347–8181. Dress: casual. Reservations necessary. AE, D, DC, MC, V. Admission: $27.95 adults, $19.95 children 3–11.*

Fort Liberty. Run by the same company that operates Mardi Gras and King Henry's Feast, this dinner show whisks you out to the Wild West, back to the days of cowboys and Indians. The entertainment is a mixed bag of real Indian dances, foot stompin' singalongs, and acrobatics. A British cowboy shows what he can do with bullwhips and lassoes, and a musician plays the *1812 Overture* on the tuba and *America the Beautiful* on an old saw (yes, the kind that cuts wood). The show is full of slapstick theatrics and country-western shindigging that children really enjoy. The chow is beef soup, fried chicken, corn-on-the-cob, and, of course, pork and beans. You are served by a rowdy chorus of cavalry recruits who keep the food coming and beverages freely pouring. All tables seat 12, so unless you are in a big party, expect to develop pass-the-ketchup relationships.

Fort Liberty completed a $25 million expansion in 1990 that added an 1870's Main Street with 20 more shops, a stockade filled with Western-themed gifts and souvenirs, and a Brave Warrior Wax Museum ($4 adults, $2 children 4–11). The ambiance is set by the photographers snapping photos of visitors who dress in cowboy garb. Forever trying to attract tourists, the Fort Liberty entertainers, including an Indian alligator wrestler, perform in the courtyard during the day. If the kids are more intent on seeing Marlboro Country than you are, go at lunch time (11–2), pick up some fast-food fried chicken for $2, and see many of the acts that are in the dinner show. *5260 W. Irlo Bronson Memorial Hwy. (U.S. 192), Kissimmee, tel. 407/*

*351–5151 or 800/347–8181. Dress: casual. Reservations neces-
sary. AE, DC, MC, V. Admission: $26.95 adults, $18.95 children 3–11.*

King Henry's Feast. Driving along the strip of hotels and shopping malls on I–4 or International Drive, you may notice two
Tudor-style buildings. One of them is the Gold Star International motel, the other is the home of Orlando's King Henry
VIII and his court of 16th-century jesters. The entertainment
includes dancers, jesters, jugglers, magicians, and singers who
encourage audience participation as King Henry celebrates his
birthday and begins a quest for his seventh bride. Saucy
wenches, who refer to customers as "me lords" and "me ladies,"
serve potato-leek soup, salad, chicken and ribs, and all the
beer, wine, and soft drinks you can guzzle. Bar drinks are extra. *8984 International Dr., Orlando, tel. 407/351–5151 or 800/
347–8181. Dress: casual. Reservations necessary. AE, D, DC,
MC, V. Admission: $26.95 adults, $18.95 children 3–11.*

Medieval Times. In a huge, modern-medieval manor house, visitors enjoy a four-course dinner while watching the struggle of
good and evil in a tournament of games, sword fights, and
jousting matches, including no less than 30 charging horses and
a cast of 75 knights, nobles, and maidens. Sounds silly? It is.
Yet if you view it through the eyes of your children, this two-
hour extravaganza of pageantry and meat-and-potatoes banquet fare can be an amusing event. Everyone faces forward
along narrow banquet tables that are stepped auditorium-style
above the tournament. If you and your family traveled the
amusement park route all day and are tired of looking at or nag-
ging at each other, you may get some respite, a bit of comic re-
lief, and possibly some vicarious pleasure from a night of
crossing lances.

Medieval Life was the result of a $2 million expansion that was
completed last year. You can watch artisans and craftsmen at
work, tour a dungeon and torture chamber, and watch an exhi-
bition featuring birds of prey. *4510 W. Irlo Bronson Memorial
Hwy. (U.S. 192), Kissimmee, tel. 407/239–0214 or 407/396–
1518; in FL, 800/432–0768; outside FL, 800/327–4024. Dress:
informal. Reservations necessary. AE, MC, V. Medieval
Times: $26 adults, $18 children 3–12; Medieval Life: $6 adults,
$4 children 3–12.*

Mark Two. This is the only true dinner theater in Orlando, with
full Broadway musicals such as *Oklahoma, My Fair Lady, West
Side Story,* and *South Pacific* staged through most of the year.
During the Christmas holiday season, shorter Broadway musical revues are presented. A buffet and full-service cocktail bar
is open for business about two hours before the show. The food
is nothing to write home about and should not be the reason to
pay a visit. The buffet of seafood Newburg, baked whitefish, a
variety of meats, and salad bar is only a few notches above cafeteria food. Best bets are the rich desserts that arrive during
intermission.

The shows are directed by the theater's owner, and the sets,
costumes, music, and choreography are all done in-house. The
actors are mostly from the Orlando area. It will not be the best
performance you will ever see, but it can be a pleasure to hear
the scores and see the routines of a favorite old musical while
you are sitting comfortably at your table with a drink in hand.

Each show runs for about six weeks, so call to see what will be playing while you are in town. There are eight shows a week, including matinees. The cost of the show, including your meal, ranges from $24–$28 for adults and $19–$23 for children (12 and under). Performances start at 8 PM Tuesday–Saturday, with 1:15 PM matinees on Wednseday and Saturday, and a 6:30 PM show on Sunday. Meals are served an hour to an hour and a half before shows. *Edgewater Center, 3376 Edgewater Dr., Orlando (from I–4 take Exit 44 and go west), tel. 407/843–6275. Dress: casual. Reservations suggested. AE, MC, V. Closed Mon.*

Church Street Station

This downtown Orlando attraction is a complete entertainment experience. Widely popular among both tourists and locals, it single-handedly began downtown Orlando's metamorphosis from a sleepy town to the nighttime hotspot it now boasts to be, and is on its way to becoming.

Until the early 1970s, Church Street offered nothing more than a dilapidated hotel, a few lifeless buildings, and a tired old train station. Attempting to convert this run-down neighborhood into a trendy entertainment complex was quite an ambitious venture.

What today is a vast complex of old fashioned saloons, dance halls, dining rooms, and shopping arcades began with just one bar—**Rosie O'Grady's.** As Rosie's popularity increased over the years, developer/owner Bob Snow acquired a neighboring building, and the complex began to spread. Now, both sides of the block are dazzlingly restored. Unlike much of what you see in Disney World, this place doesn't just look authentic—it *is* authentic. The train on the tracks is an actual 19th-century steam engine; the whistling calliope was especially rebuilt to blow its original tunes. Just about everything down to the cobblestones that clatter under the horse-drawn carriages are the real McCoy. Buildings have been completely redecorated with collectibles and memorabilia from around the world; look carefully at the details and don't be shy about asking where something came from. You may be surprised to discover that a beautiful mahogany phone booth is actually a confessional that was salvaged from a French monastery.

You can spend an evening in part of the complex, or you can wander from area to area, soaking up the peculiar characteristics of each. For a single admission price of $14.95 (adults) or $9.95 (4–12), you're permitted to wander freely, stay as long as you wish, and do what you want, whether it's drinking, dancing, dining, or people-watching. Food and drink cost extra and are not cheap, but they add to the fun. Parts of the complex are open during the day, but the place is usually quiet then; the pace picks up at night, especially on weekends, with crowds thickest from 10 to 11. The streets can get insanely busy at these times, but it's all part of the spirit of bustling good fun that continues into the night. *129 W. Church St., Orlando, tel. 407/422–2434. Dress: casual. Reservations not necessary. AE, MC, V.*

Rosie O'Grady's Good Time Emporium. This is a turn-of-the-century saloon with dark wood, brass trim, a full Dixieland band blaring out of a gazebo, counter-top can-can dancers, tap dancers, and vaudeville singers. Is this a set for *The Music Man* or an evening at the Moulin Rouge? It's difficult at first to tell. The 90-minute shows begin at 7:30 PM. The last show starts at midnight. Multidecker sandwiches and hot dogs are sold in the Gay 90s Sandwich Parlour from 4:30 PM till 11 PM.

Apple Annie's Courtyard. This is a relatively quiet—some would say flairless—nook that features continuous live folk and bluegrass music from about 8 PM to 2 PM. It's a good place to rest your feet, have a drink, and people-watch. Salads, fruit platters, and exotic drinks are served from 11 PM to 2 PM.

Lili Marlene's Aviator's Pub and Restaurant. Here you have a relaxed, wood-paneled English pub atmosphere and the finest dining on Church Street. Food is hearty, upscale, and very American—mostly steaks, ribs, and seafood. Prices are not cheap. The walls have biplane-era memorabilia, and a large-scale model aircraft hangs from the ceiling. Open for lunch 11–4, and dinner 5:30–midnight.

Phineas Phogg's Balloon Works. This is a very popular, happening disco filled with young singles over 21 and a sprinkling of old-timers showing off their moves on the dance floor. It has a good-looking yuppie tourist crowd, leavened with locals. Contemporary dance tunes are played on a sound system that will blow your argyle socks off. The place is jammed by midnight and open until 2. Much of the young crowd feels it is worth the price of admission into the Station just to be able to come here.

Orchid Garden Ballroom and Dessert Cafe. Decorative lamps, iron latticework, arched ceilings, and stained-glass windows create a striking Victorian arcade where visitors sit, drink, and listen to a first-rate band pounding out popular tunes from the 1950s to present. Open until 2 AM.

Cracker's Oyster Bar. Located behind the Orchid Garden, Cracker's is a good place to get a quick gumbo or chowder fix and slam down a few oysters with a beer chaser, or make a selection from one of the largest wine cellars in Florida. Open until midnight.

Cheyenne Saloon and Opera House. This is the biggest, fanciest, rootin'-tootin' saloon you may ever see. The former triple-level opera house is covered with moose racks, steer horns, buffalo heads, and Remington rifles; and there is a seven-piece country-western band that darn near brings the house down. This is a fun crowd to watch with all the pickin', strummin', fiddlin', hollerin', and do-see-doin'. Make sure you come equipped with your best stompin' shoes, cowboy hat, and catcalls. An upstairs restaurant serves chicken-and-ribs saloon fare. The shows start at 8:30, 10, and 11:30, and 1 AM.

Church Street Station Exchange. The newest addition to the complex, near Church Street Station, is a razzle-dazzle marketplace filled with more than 50 specialty shops and restaurants on the first two floors. The third floor has been taken over by **Commander Ragtime's Midway of Fun, Food and Games.** The Exchange is free and open 11 AM–2 AM. The shops close by 11 PM.

Bars and Clubs

The bars and nightclubs have been divided into two sections. The first covers the tourist hotel districts in the Disney area, including Kissimmee, Lake Buena Vista, and International Drive. These places are usually filled with visitors to Walt Disney World. The other section covers the city of Orlando and Winter Park, both of which cater to a more local crowd. Remember that clubs on Disney property are allowed to stay open later than bars elsewhere, and many of them don't have last call until 2:45 AM.

Disney Area **Little Darlin's Rock n' Roll Palace.** Shake, rattle, and roll the night away in this 1950s and '60s nostalgia nightclub. The interior looks like an opera house, and there's an orchestra pit dance floor and a huge bandstand stage featuring famous old rock bands that still tour, such as The Drifters and The Platters. The crowd is a mix of young and old, singles and couples. The club features a very talented house band that serves up live music seven nights a week. Much of the menu is vintage '50s: hot dogs, cheese steak sandwiches, and banana splits, but there is also prime rib. *Old Town, 5770 Spacecoast Pkwy., Kissimmee 34746, tel. 407/396-6499 or 407/827-6169. Dress: casual. Open noon–2 AM. Admission: $8.50.*

Giraffe Lounge. Located inside the Hotel Royal Plaza in WDW Village at Lake Buena Vista, this flashy disco with spinning, colored lights is usually densely packed on weekends. It is a small place, and classy it ain't, but there's a lot going on, including live bands five nights a week. Happy hour runs daily from 4 to 9:30 PM. Music plays and the bartender pours until 3 AM. *Hotel Royal Plaza, WDW Village, Lake Buena Vista, tel. 407/828-2828. Dress: casual. Open 4 PM–3 AM. No cover charge.*

The Laughing Kookaburra. A big hotel nightclub with live band music nightly and a serious singles crowd of all ages. The music is loud and the dance floor can get very crowded—a plus for some, a minus for others. The bar serves up 99 brands of beer, plus cocktails. Happy hour with free bar food runs daily from 4 to 8 PM. Live bands play five nights a week, and a Talent Showcase takes over on Sunday. *Buena Vista Palace Hotel, WDW Village, Lake Buena Vista, tel. 407/827-3520. Dress: casual. All major credit cards. Open 4 PM–3 AM. No cover charge.*

Bennigan's. A young singles spot that draws crowds in the early evening and during happy hours from 4 to 7 PM and from 11 PM to 2 AM. It caters mostly to nontourists who work in the area. Food is served almost until closing. *6324 International Dr., Orlando, tel. 407/351-4436. Open 11 AM–2 AM.*

Orlando Area The nightclubs in Orlando have significantly more character than those in the Disney hotel area. If you have the energy to get in your car, you will probably find these spots more satisfying and less touristy—if you can find them.

J.J. Whispers. A classy, brassy singles crowd flocks to this trendy disco, which tries hard to maintain an image of cosmopolitan class. Expect to mingle with fashion-conscious locals in their tastefully outrageous attire. The club is equally popular with the over-30 set, who listen to music from the 1940s, '50s, and '60s in the Showroom. The young people do what young people do in a massive, multilevel, state-of-the-art disco. J.J.'s has one restaurant serving bar-food fare, and another, that is open for lunch and sometimes features comedians, magicians, and other stage acts. It is also home to Bonkerz, a comedy club featuring professional network and cable television comics. Live entertainment (Tues.–Sun., 8 PM–2 AM) includes all-male and all-female revues and live bands. *5100 Adanson St., Orlando, tel. 407/629–4779. Dress: tasteful but outrageous—or just a jacket. AE, MC, V. Cover: $5 and up; $10 and up for Bonkerz, tel. 407/629–2665. To get there, take I–4 to the Lee Rd. exit and go west for about ½ mi on Lee Rd. Watch for a sharp left-hand turn at Adanson St. J.J.'s is located at the end of the Lee Rd. Shopping Center.*

Crocodile Club. This bar, inside a restaurant called Bailey's in Winter Park, collects a young, well-dressed college crowd from neighboring Rollins College. The atmosphere is more sophisticated and yuppified than most Orlando bars. Expect to hear jazz and Motown and dance to pop. *Bailey's Restaurant, 118 W. Fairbanks Ave., Winter Park, tel. 407/647–8501.*

Sullivan's Trailways Lounge. A very popular place with much right-friendly charm where people of all ages and many families come to strut their stuff on the largest dance floor in Florida. Even Yankees are welcome in this southern country-western dance hall. Big name performers entertain on occasion; local bands play Tuesday–Saturday. *1108 S. Orange Blossom Trail (U.S. 441), tel. 407/843–2934. Bands play 8 PM–2 AM. Cover charge: $2 and up.*

Beacham's Blue Note. This classy restaurant club in downtown Orlando offers local jazz and blues and occasional national acts. *54 N. Orange Ave., tel. 407/843–3078. Open nightly. Cover charge: $3 and up.*

Big Bang. A small, imaginatively Bohemian downtown night spot with a trendy but friendly atmosphere. The club, which features a mix of music from alternative to rap, keeps it pretty funky on weekends and has themes on weekday evenings. It is open after hours for dancing, coffee, and mineral water. Be sure to check out the Winnebago Room. *102 N. Orange Ave., tel. 407/425–9277. Open Fri.–Sat. 10 PM–4 AM; Tues. 10 PM–3 AM, Disco Hell; Wed. 9 PM–2:30 AM, Coffeehouse; Thurs. 10 PM–3 AM, International Music. Cover charge: $2 on weekends.*

10   The Cocoa Beach Area

More and more visitors to central Florida are discovering that the Space Coast beaches offer an attractive excursion after a vacation full of theme park touring. Less than an hour from Orlando, Cocoa Beach Area, Brevard County, is a popular spot for families because it combines water sports, cruises, and a sandy beach with inland pleasures such as Spaceport U.S.A., shopping, and sports. Cocoa Beach is also the best place to view shuttle launches and spectacular sunsets.

Important Addresses and Phone Numbers

Visitor Information
Brevard County Tourist Development Council (2235 N. Courtenay Pkwy., Merritt Island, Fl. 32953, tel. 800/USA–1969 or 407/453–2211).

Launch information (tel. 900/321–LIFTOFF—the call will cost 75 cents).

Tourism & Convention Council, Cocoa Beach Area Chamber of Commerce (400 Fortenberry Rd., Merritt Island, Fl. 32952; tel. 407/452–4390 or 407/452–2200).

24-hour Emergency Care
Cape Canaveral Hospital (701 Cocoa Beach Causeway [S.R. 520], Cocoa Beach, tel. 407/799–7111).

Language Bank (tel. 407/452–4390 or 407/459–2200).

Getting Around

The Beeline Expressway is the most direct route from Orlando International Airport to most of the attractions. Get off the Beeline (Hwy. 528) at Hwy. 520 to go into Cocoa Beach. Stay on the Beeline if traveling to Port Canaveral. If you are heading toward Spaceport U.S.A., follow signs to Kennedy Space Center and *not* to Cape Canaveral.

Exploring the Cocoa Beach Area

Spaceport USA at the **Kennedy Space Center** is free, making it perhaps the best entertainment bargain in Florida. You can stroll through an outdoor rocket garden with authentic rockets and tour a museum filled with spacecraft that have explored the last frontier. There are also two bus tours: One takes visitors to see some of NASA's current launch facilities, including the Space Shuttle launch. Another bus goes to Cape Canaveral Air Force Station, where you can trace the history of the early space program. Understandably, some visitors are less than thrilled about viewing the space program framed through a bus window. There is both live and recorded narration, but most sights are experienced from afar, except for historical exhibits at camera stops.

For a close-up at how space-related products have affected our daily lives, see "Satellites and You." The free multimedia presentation is hosted by an animatronic crew, who take visitors through a simulated space station. The one event that should make your entire trip to Spaceport worthwhile (if you have not already experienced it at the Air and Space Museum in Washington, DC) is the IMAX film *The Dream Is Alive*. Projected onto a five-and-a-half story screen, this 40-minute film takes you from astronaut training through a thundering shuttle launch, into the cabins and life on board the shuttle during

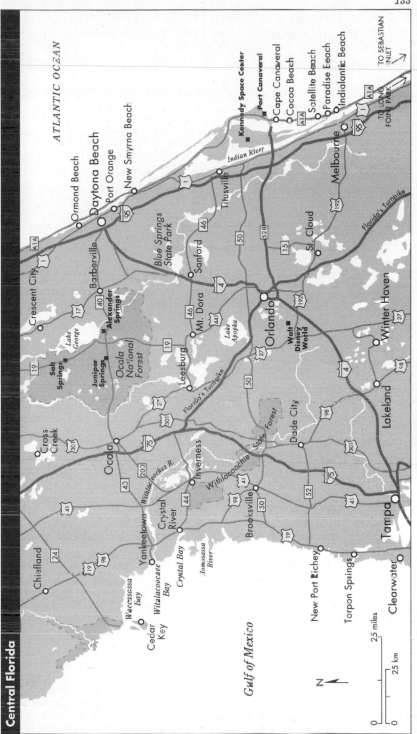

Central Florida

flight, back to Earth for touchdown. The footage shot by the astronauts themselves will leave you breathless. It is a completely overwhelming experience, costing only a few dollars for the whole family. *Kennedy Space Center, FL 32899, tel. 407/ 452–2121 or 800/432–2153. Bus tours: $6 adults, $3 children 3– 12. IMAX film: $2.75 adults, $1.75 children. No credit cards. Open daily 9 AM–dark. Last tour 2 hours before dark. Closed Christmas Day and certain launch dates. Kennedy Space Center is about a 90-minute drive from Disney World and a 60-minute drive from Orlando. To get there, take the Beeline Expressway (off I-4) east for about 25 min. to Rte. 407. Go east to Rte. 405, then east again, following signs to Spaceport. Parking and kennel facilities are free.*

At the entrance to Spaceport USA is a new museum, **United States Astronaut Hall of Fame,** where you can view videotapes of historical moments in the space program. *Follow Kennedy Space Center signs to hwy. 405. The U.S. Astronaut Hall of Fame and U.S. Space Camp are one block east of U.S. 1. Tel. 407/269–6100. Admission: $4.95 adults, $2.95 children 3–12. Open daily 8–7.*

To see what the area was like before the space program arrived, visit **The Brevard Museum of History and Natural Science.** Don't overlook one of the best hands-on discovery rooms or the Taylor Collection of Victorian-era memorabilia. The nature center has 22 acres of trails encompassing three ecological systems of Florida. *Take U.S. 1 to Michigan Avenue, turn west and follow the signs. Tel. 407/632–1830. Admission: $2 adults, $1 senior citizens and students, children free under 5. Open Tues.–Sat. 10–4, Sun. 1–4, closed Mon.*

Port Canaveral, on the southern end of **Cape Canaveral,** is home to *Europa Cruise Line* (tel. 407/799–0449 or 800/688–PLAY), which depards on daily one-day cruises into the Atlantic, and **Premier Cruise Lines** (tel. 800/327–7113), offering three- and four-night cruises to the Bahamas, departing Monday, Thursday, and Friday.

Port Canaveral also is the site of annual surfing championships, thanks to the well-formed Atlantic waves that wash the beaches between **Cocoa Beach** and **Sebastian Inlet. Ron Jon's Surf Shop** (4151 N. Atlantic Ave., Cocoa Beach, tel. 407/799–8820) is almost an attraction in itself, with its massive collection of swim wear, beach gear, and T-shirts. Beach bikes and other water sports equipment are available for rent.

To the south is Cocoa Beach. When looking for a place to park your beach umbrella, keep in mind that Cocoa Beach is more crowded than the beaches farther south, such as **Satellite Beach, Indialantic,** and **Melbourne Beach.**

A good way to become acquainted with the area's waterways is to take a sightseeing or dinner cruise on *The Little River Queen,* which departs daily from **Gatsby's Dockside** in Cocoa Beach. You'll see everything from elegant residential areas to native wildlife—dolphins, manatees, and wading birds. *Two-hour sightseeing cruises depart daily at 2 PM ($8 adults, $4 children under 12), 2½-hour dinner cruises leave Sun.–Thurs. at 6:30 PM ($18 adults, $8 children under 12), and a 3½-hour Dixieland Jazz and dinner cruise casts off Fri. and Sat. at 7 PM ($26 adults, $13 children under 12). 500 W. Cocoa Beach*

Causeway, Cocoa Beach, tel. 407/783–2380. Reservations are advised for dinner cruises.

Exploring **Olde Cocoa Village** (201 Michigan Ave., Cocoa, tel. 407/632–1830 or 407/639–3500) may convince you that there was life in Cocoa before the space program. Cobblestone walkways thread through this landscaped cluster of restored 1890s buildings in downtown Cocoa, where specialty shops display pottery, macrame, leather and silvercraft, afghans, fine art, and fashions; and horse-drawn carriages can take you for a ride through a village. The **Cocoa Village Playhouse** (tel. 407/636–5050) community theater is based here and provides regular entertainment.

Sebastian Inlet marks the southern boundary of this region east of Orlando. Two recreational areas ensure the preservation of some great fishing grounds and beaches. If you like to camp, check out **Long Point Park** (tel. 407/732–3839) and **Sebastian Inlet State Recreation Area** (tel. 407/984–4852); both are near Melbourne Beach in the south end of Brevard County.

Beaches

On the mid-Atlantic coast, between Ormond Beach and Sebastian Inlet, are about 100 miles of sandy beaches accessible to the public. The only beach area closed to the public borders the space center on Cape Canaveral. Choice beaches and parks are listed below.

Canaveral National Seashore (tel. 904/428–3384), just east of New Smyrna Beach on Rte. A1A, is a 57,000-acre park that is home to more than 250 kinds of birds and animals. The remote beach bordering the Atlantic is noted for its sand dunes and seashells. A self-guided hiking trail leads to the top of an Indian shell midden at Turtle Mound, where picnic tables are available. Free brochures and maps are available at the Visitor Center on Rte. A1A.
Paradise Beach (tel. 407/779–4008), a scenic 10-acre park north of Indialantic on Rte. A1A, has 1,600 feet of beach, picnic facilities, grills, showers, restrooms, and a refreshment stand. A lifeguard is on duty during the summer. There is a fee for parking, and picnic tables must be reserved in advance.
Sebastian Inlet State Recreation Area (tel. 407/984–4852), about 12 miles south of Melbourne on Rte. A1A, offers three miles of beachfront for swimming, surfing, snorkeling, and scuba diving. The 576-acre park also features bathhouse facilities, campsites, a food concession, fishing jetty, and boat ramp.

Sports

Biking In Cocoa Beach, rent bicycles from **Ron Jon's Surf Shop** (4151 N. Atlantic Ave., tel. 407/799–8820).

Fishing You can deep-sea troll in the Atlantic for blue and white marlin, sailfish, dolphin, king mackerel, tuna, and wahoo. Grouper, red snapper, and amberjack are deep-sea bottom fishing prizes. Surf casting is popular for pompano, bluefish, flounder, and sea bass. From fishing piers, anglers pull in sheepshead, mackerel, trout, and tarpon. Most Atlantic beach communities have a lighted pier with bait-and-tackle shop and rest rooms. Deep-sea charters are found at Port Canaveral. Call ahead for prices and reservations: **Cape Marina** (800 Scallop Dr., Port Canaveral, tel. 407/783–8410); **Miss Cape Canaveral** (630 Glen Cheek Dr., Port Canaveral, tel. 407/783–5274 or 407/648–2211 from Orlando); **Pelican Princess** (665 Glen Cheek Dr., Port Canaveral, tel. 407/784–3474, Brevard County; 407/843–3474, Orlando).

Golfing **Cocoa Beach Municipal Golf Course** (5000 Tom Warringer Blvd., Cocoa Beach, tel. 407/783–4911) has 6,968 yards open to the public.

Dining

Moderate prices and fresh seafood are characteristic of Cocoa Beach dining. Here is a sampling of some favorites.

American **Mango Tree Restaurant.** Candles, fresh flowers, white linen tablecloths, rattan basket chairs with fluffy cushions, and eggshell-color walls adorned with tropical watercolors by local artists set a romantic mood at the Mango Tree. The intimate dining room overlooks a garden aviary that is home to exotic doves and pheasants. Try the grouper broiled and topped with scallops, shrimp, and hollandaise sauce. *Cottage Row, 118 N. Atlantic Ave., Cocoa Beach, tel. 407/799–0513. Dress: casual. Reservations advised. AE, MC, V. Expensive.*
Spinnaker's. At this entertainment center, set on an 800-foot pier extending into the ocean, visitors can find a boutique, fishing bait, and dining ranging from mesquite-grilled alligator snacks at a boardwalk bar to coconut beer shrimp at the Pier House, which serves dinner 5–10 PM. *401 Meade Avenue, Cocoa Beach, tel. 407/783–7549. Dress: casual. Reservations required. AE, DC, MC, V. Moderate–Expensive.*
Gatsby's Food and Spirits. This casual waterfront spot serves up prime rib, steaks, and seafood. Early-bird special dinner prices are in effect between 4:30 and 6:30. *480 W. Cocoa Beach Causeway, Cocoa Beach, tel. 407/783–2380. Dress: casual. Reservations advised. AE, DC, MC, V. Moderate.*

Italian **Alma's Italian Restaurant.** Five crowded, noisy dining rooms keep the waitresses busy. The specialties of the house are veal marsala and more than 200 imported and domestic wines. *306 N. Orlando Ave., Cocoa Beach, tel. 407/783–1981. Dress: casual. Reservations advised. AE, DC, MC, V. Inexpensive.*

Seafood **Bernard's Surf.** Don't come to Bernard's for the view; there are no windows in the two main dining rooms. Come for steaks and local fish and a few unusual dishes like alligator and buffalo. Try Snapper à la Doris, a fish house specialty. Rusty's Raw Bar is new and offers 20 different seafood dishes or burger and fries for landlubbers. *2 S. Atlantic Ave., Cocoa Beach, tel. 407/783–2401. Dress: casual. Reservations advised. AE, DC, MC, V. Closed Christmas. Expensive.*

Lodging

Many of the hotels in the Cocoa Beach area have weekend packages that offer significantly lower rates. Frequently included are cocktails, meals, or admission tickets to nightclubs.

Holiday Inn Cocoa Beach Resort. When two separate beach hotels were redesigned and a promenade park landscaped between them, the Holiday Inn Cocoa Beach Resort was born. It

features plush modern public rooms, an olympi
pool, tennis courts, and private access to the h
choose from a wide selection of accommodations
king, and oceanfront suites; villas; and bilevel lofts—all with
in-room movies. Free aerobic workouts are offered, as are
planned activities for children. *1300 N. Atlantic Ave., Cocoa
Beach 32931, tel. 407/783–2271. 500 rooms. AE, DC, MC, V.
Expensive.*

Crossway Inn. Located across the street from the ocean and
within walking distance of at least 16 restaurants, this is a convenient lodging. You can choose from standard double rooms,
minisuites, or fully equipped efficiencies—all are clean, comfortable, and decorated with light tropical colors. Amenities
include a lighted volleyball court, a 15-foot "mallet pool" court
(you sink the 8-ball with a croquet mallet), a children's playground, and an airy Key West-style lounge with rattan furnishings and hand-painted tropical murals. *3901 N. Atlantic Ave.,
Cocoa Beach 32931, tel. 407/783–2221; in FL, 800/247–2221,
outside FL, 800/327–2224. 94 units. AE, DC, MC, V. Inexpensive.*

Pelican Landing Resort On the Ocean. This recently refurbished, beachfront, two-story gray motel conveys a friendly atmosphere with its oceanfront views and screened porches
(available in Units 1 and 6). Microwaves in each room, board-
walks to the beach, picnic tables, and a gas grill round out the
amenities. *1201 S. Atlantic Ave., Cocoa Beach 32931, tel. 407/
783–7197. 11 units. MC, V. Inexpensive.*

Nightlife

Coconuts. The Saturday bikini contests and the April Jet-ski
rodeo, along with Mr. Muscle contests and dirt-in-the-face volleyball, attract the under-40 set to this oceanside nightspot.
Patrons dance to live music most evenings, and there is a dining
area. *2 Minuteman Causeway, tel. 407/784–1422. Open Mon.–
Sat. 11:30 AM–2 AM; Sun. 11:30 AM–midnight.*

Plum's Lounge/Holiday Inn Cocoa Beach. This lounge features
dancing and live entertainment nightly. There is a beach dock
on the ocean and a bar by the pool. *1300 N. Atlantic Ave., Cocoa Beach, tel. 407/783–2271. Open noon–1:30 AM.*

Index

Index